Transition toolkit

A framework for managing change and successful transition planning for children and young people with autism spectrum conditions

Edited by Karen Broderick and
Tina Mason-Williams

SECOND EDITION

British Library Cataloguing in Publication Data

A CIP record for this book is available from the Public Library

© BILD Publications 2005, 2008
Second edition 2008

BILD Publications is the imprint of:
British Institute of Learning Disabilities
Campion House
Green Street
Kidderminster
Worcestershire DY10 1JL

Telephone: 01562 723010
Fax: 01562 723029
E-mail: enquiries@bild.org.uk

Website: www.bild.org.uk

With the exception of the templates in Section 6, no part of this publication may be reproduced without prior permission from the publisher, except for the quotation of brief passages for review, teaching or reference purposes, when an acknowledgment of the source must be given.

ISBN: 978 1 905218 05 9

Printed in the UK by Latimer Trend & Company Ltd, Plymouth

BILD publications are distributed by:
BookSource
50 Cambuslang Road
Cambuslang
Glasgow G32 8NB

Telephone: 0845 370 0067
Fax: 0845 370 0064

For a publications catalogue with details of all BILD books and journals telephone 01562 723010, e-mail enquiries@bild.org.uk or visit the BILD website www.bild.org.uk

About the British Institute of Learning Disabilities

The British Institute of Learning Disabilities is committed to improving the quality of life for people with a learning disability by involving them and their families in all aspects of our work, working with government and public bodies to achieve full citizenship, undertaking beneficial research and development projects and helping service providers to develop and share good practice.

Acknowledgements

The advisory group would like to thank the following for contributing to the text of the first edition of Transition toolkit:

    Elizabeth Attfield, autism.west midlands

    Sue Briggs, freelance educational consultant

    Ann Croft, teacher in charge, Beaconside Autism Resource Base

    Alison Riddell, Access and Inclusion Service

    Clare Smith, parent

The advisory group would also like to thank the following for commenting on and/or trialling the Transition toolkit:

    Integrated Services – Specialist Support, Autism Team

    Charford First School

    Jane Hunt, specialist teaching assistant, Beaconside Autism Resource Base

    Lickey Hills Primary School, Language Unit

    Parents of pupils from Beaconside and Catshill Schools

    The Vale of Evesham School

    Tim Garey, student

    Walkwood Middle School, Autism Resource Base

Transition toolkit advisory group

Elizabeth Attfield	autism.west midlands
Lesley Barcham	British Institute of Learning Disabilities
Karen Broderick	principal teacher, Autism, Integrated Services – Specialist Support, Worcestershire
Ann Croft	Beaconside Autism Resource Base, Worcestershire
Ann Diprose	British Institute of Learning Disabilities
Sue Hatton	autism.west midlands
Melanie Henderson	headteacher, Catshill First School, Worcestershire
Tina Mason-Williams	parent/SEN governor
Reg Moore	primary inspector, School Improvement and Achievement Division, Worcestershire
Kathy Roberts	policy and development manager, Services to Schools Division, Worcestershire

Contents

Section 1	Introduction	7
Section 2	The transition plan and example templates with notes	17
Section 3	How to use the templates – case study examples	31
Section 4	Strategies and guidelines for successful transitions	53
Section 5	Further reading and references	77
Section 6	Templates	95

Section 1

Introduction

In this section you will find:

- background information concerning the development of the *Transition toolkit*
- the key features of autism spectrum conditions (ASC)
- why young people with an ASC may find change problematic
- the definition of transition
- the purpose of the toolkit
- the statutory context
- types of change and transitions that occur in everyday life and that require careful planning for young people with an ASC

Background

This toolkit came from a project that reviewed current practice in schools at times of transition for children and young people with an autism spectrum condition (ASC). It has been revised to take account of developments since the first edition and to make it even easier to use. The project's advisory group oversaw the review of practice in participating schools.

The toolkit was compiled in partnership with:
- individuals with an autism spectrum condition (ASC)
- parents/carers of young people with an ASC
- British Institute of Learning Disabilities (BILD)
- Integrated Services Specialist Support Autism Team, Worcestershire County Council
- Beaconside Primary and Catshill First School, Worcestershire
- autism west midlands

The project was funded by the DfES Small Programmes Fund 2003–04 and managed by BILD.

This toolkit is for:
- staff who work in educational establishments
- local authority (LA) support services
- young people with an ASC and their families
- professionals from other agencies

There are a wide range of terms to describe young people with autism and related conditions. The use of the term autism spectrum condition (ASC) in this toolkit refers to children and young people with autism, Asperger syndrome, semantic and/or pragmatic difficulties and related conditions.

The term autism spectrum condition is used instead of autism spectrum disorder to reflect current thinking of some leading specialists in the field of autism, such as Christopher Gillberg and Tony Attwood (2004). Indeed, many people with Asperger syndrome have stated that they prefer the use of the phrase as they do not believe they are 'disordered' but just differently ordered.

The aim is to move away from the negative connotations of a 'disorder' and to reflect the view that individuals with an ASC experience and perceive the world differently from people of typical neurological development and that it is the 'neuro-typical' world which contributes to the many challenges they face.

The stakeholders in the transition process are all of those involved that may be negatively or positively affected by the process.

Key features of autism spectrum conditions

Many people with ASCs have written personal accounts (Grandin, 1995; Jackson, 2002; Lawson, 2001; Sainsbury, 2000). Two of the outstanding messages from these descriptions are:

- that there are many strengths or gifts associated with having an ASC, as well as difficulties
- that people with an ASC experience the world and think differently from people of typical neurological development. It is therefore helpful to think of the challenges and difficulties that people with an ASC face in everyday life.

ASC is a lifelong, complex difficulty. A child with an ASC becomes an adult with an ASC.

People with an ASC demonstrate, to a greater or lesser degree, difficulties in the development of three key areas, often referred to as the 'triad of Impairments' as described by Lorna Wing (1996):

- *communication*: in learning to talk, in understanding others, and in making others understand one's own needs, in the use and understanding of body language and facial expressions
- *socialisation*: with initiating and maintaining appropriate social relationships, with understanding the rules of reciprocal social interaction
- *imagination*: with rigid and inflexible thinking which may lead to a resistance to change, an insistence on set routines and repetitive behaviours

In addition, there may also be present:

- sensory issues, either an over-or under-reaction to sights, sounds, touch, smells, taste or other sensations
- sense of balance and sense of self in space may be impaired
- motor difficulties, leading to problems in motor planning and self organisation

Sensory processing – that which we see, hear, smell, feel and taste – gives us the information to make sense of the environment and ourselves. Our central nervous system receives, interprets, organises, filters and sends messages to the rest of our body.

There is clear scientific research (Myles et al, 2000) which supports the view that people with an ASC may experience difficulties with ineffective sensory processing and sensory integration.

These sensory difficulties have a huge impact on a person's ability to interface with any situation, another individual or activity. The recording of personal accounts from individuals with an ASC has led to a better understanding of their perception of the world and the difficulties they experience. It has also given us an insight into the individuality of the sensory profile for a person with an ASC. Thus, when planning any programme or development, especially transition planning, it is essential to assess and identify any specific sensory issues and to adjust the environment and situations accordingly.

A diagnosis of an ASC is often not made on its own; there may be other medical conditions which are associated with it. These conditions are termed co-morbid conditions. They exist alongside an ASC, yet are separate medical issues which each have their own unique characteristics. Very often the presenting behaviours or symptoms that are seen are so intertwined that considerable investigation is required to understand where these behaviours are coming from. This can, of course, make life more complicated.

Individuals with an ASC often have complex needs and if there is also a co-morbid condition present, this will clearly influence that person's overall needs at times of transition and at all other times.

There are many excellent publications which describe what an ASC is and the reader is signposted to the further reading and references in Section 5 for more details. Publications that give a good introduction to ASC are highlighted by an asterisk.

Why young people with an ASC may find change problematic

All the previously mentioned potential difficulties lead to many challenges for people with an ASC. One area which is particularly problematic is that of coping with change and the need for sameness and routine to support their understanding of daily events.

This difficulty coping with change can perhaps best be illustrated and explained by an example. A pupil with an ASC in Year 2 follows a set routine on coming into school which is supported by visual cue cards:

- Hang your coat up.
- Take your lunch box, drink bottle and water bottle out of your bag.
- Put your drink and lunch box on the shelf in the classroom.
- Put your water bottle on your table.
- Put your reading folder in your drawer.
- Sit down in your seat and listen to the teacher.

One morning after the rest of the class are sitting down, the teacher finds this pupil alone in the corridor seemingly unable to move and very distressed. Overnight the builders had been in and moved the mobile peg racks to the other side of the corridor. All the other children had 'seen' the change and just hung their coats up on their usual pegs, then carried on with the rest of their usual routine. The inability of the child with an ASC to understand and cope with this minor change is one example of the rigid and inflexible thinking of individuals with ASCs. It can be broken down as follows:

- Children and young people with an ASC find difficulty seeing the whole picture, instead seeing each individual part of a situation, without the ability to bring all of this information together. The child does not see 'coming into school in the morning' as one event with a series of steps designed to ensure you are ready to start the lesson, even though he is in his third year of school. The child focuses on each individual part without seeing the end result. So he needs prompts and schedules, such as the cue cards referred to in the example, to start and to carry out the actions required to get him ready for the day.

- So what happens if an element of the situation changes – the coat pegs move? To this young person it is a new situation. He does not have the flexibility of thought to look around for the pegs and then carry on with his normal routine. For him, it is a completely different situation. What he needs is a very specific individual prompt from the teacher to show him where his peg has gone. It may then take several days before the new position of the pegs becomes familiar.

The following year this pupil moves to Year 3 in a different part of the school. Can he generalise his knowledge of coming into school into the new situation by using his coming into school schedule? Yes, probably, but only after each individual part of the routine has been explained, and more importantly, shown to him in advance and for several times at the beginning of term. He will not be able to 'make sense of the whole' as quickly as the other children.

Changes occur naturally many times every hour, day, week or month. The difficulty of individuals with an ASC to see the whole, to think their way through minor changes and to generalise their experience to new situations means that these everyday changes and transitions, which most people deal with automatically, can be confusing and often traumatic experiences for young people with an ASC.

In our example, when the pegs are moved, the child may not understand, or have the communication skills to explain to the teacher, why he is bewildered. He may also be overwhelmed by the increased noise levels from the other children, excited by the arrival of the builders, etc. So any change can trigger stress and anxiety that may result in behaviours that are difficult to manage. However, as the example shows, there are proven techniques and strategies that are effective in dealing with change and facilitating successful transitions.

Definition of transition

Transition is defined as 'passing or change from one place, state or condition to another'.

There are many changes that occur in everyday life and they all involve transition. For the reasons outlined previously, any minor or major changes in routines, rules, personnel or procedures may prove problematic. The rigidity of thought processes, sensory processing issues and communication difficulties experienced by young people with an ASC means that all minor and major transitions require careful and systematic planning.

When young people have been given the opportunity to express what is important to them in the transition process, the overwhelming message that comes across is the need for the young person to 'say goodbye' and to have some kind of closure to that phase of their life. Closure is just as important to the child and young person with an ASC, to provide a marker between one stage and another. This may take many forms and will be very individual to the person, but will certainly need to be included in the planning and preparation.

The purpose of the toolkit

Young people with an ASC are able to manage change successfully as long as those changes are clearly explained in ways that they understand. They require appropriate visual aids to support understanding and in advance of the changes occurring. The purpose of this toolkit is to:

- form part of a whole school approach to achieving inclusion of all pupils
- form part of a whole school approach to managing change and transition
- identify examples of change and transition to aid planning
- provide information and advice towards achieving seamless transitions
- trigger ideas and prompt discussion in the development of transition plans
- identify who the stakeholders are and who should be consulted and involved in the process
- identify resources useful to support the transition plan
- provide templates for use in the planning process
- provide case studies as examples of how to use the transition framework

The key to successful use of the toolkit and hence seamless transitions is to ensure communication between all stakeholders and to keep the young person with an ASC central to the whole planning process.

The statutory context

The Disability Discrimination Act 1995, as subsequently amended, applies to the education of pupils, the employment of staff and the provision of services to other school users. Part 5a of the Act, which came into force in December 2006, imposes a disability equality duty on schools and a requirement to draw up a disability equality scheme to demonstrate how the school is fulfilling the duty. One key element of the duty is the requirement to take account of disabilities even if this involves treating people with a disability more favourably. Implementing effective transition planning for pupils with an ASC as part of the school's disability equality scheme action plan is a very effective way of taking account of the disabilities of those pupils at times of transition.

In addition, under the Act, reasonable adjustments should be embedded into school practice to take account of different learning styles of pupils with disabilities, including those with ASC. Examples of reasonable adjustments include:

- visual prompts and cues, eg objectives for each lesson put on the board
- provision of calm areas with low levels of stimuli (eg no wall displays, etc) for pupils with ASC to have time out
- removal of flickering fluorescent lights to reduce visual disturbance

The Special Educational Needs (SEN) Code of Practice (DfES, 2001) focuses on transition planning for pupils in Year 9 and above. This toolkit is intended for use with pupils experiencing a much broader range of transitions. Some examples of the types of transition which may occur in the school environment are shown in Figure 1.

Figure 1: Types of transition

```
         Home              Early years
                           placement
                                              Lesson
                                                ↓
                                              Lesson
Change of
transport
                    School
                                              Year class
Daily activity                                   ↓
    ↓                                         Year class
Daily activity


Specialist placement      School         Mainstream placement
        ↓                                          ↓
Mainstream placement                     Specialist placement
```

Note: Specialist placement includes special schools, mainstream autism bases within mainstream schools and language units

Section 2

The transition plan and example templates with notes

In this section you can find out about:
- what a transition plan is and what it should achieve
- the transition templates

The transition plan

A transition plan is a detailed plan to attain a successful change or passage from one state or stage to another.

> 'The transition plan should draw together information from a range of individuals in order to plan coherently with the young person for their transition.'
> (SEN *Code of Practice*, 2002)

This reference relates to the pupil with a statement of special educational need as defined by the SEN Code of Practice, and the requirements for their Year 9 transition review. However this quotation is relevant for all other types of transition planning and for pupils of any ability with an ASC.

For success, there should be a clear and easy-to-follow route through the transition plan and process.

The transition templates

The templates in this toolkit form a framework to help you to write your transition plan. It is intended that the templates selected will match the individual's needs. *It is not intended for all templates to be used for all changes and transitions.* Small daily changes and changes to established routines may only require a new or revised schedule or set of cue cards. A move to a new school may require a transition plan incorporating some or all the templates, supported by a range of visual aids in a form appropriate for the individual child or young person to fully comprehend.

The selected templates will form part of the transition plan. The templates and strategies identified are not exhaustive but merely a recipe of support to be considered and accessed.

The completed transition plan should also be passed on to the receiving school or class as this automatically provides key information in an easy-to-access format.

The following templates are included:

- pupil profile
- summary of transition and key stakeholders
- identified training needs and support for staff
- pupil information relevant to the transition
- key strategies and resources for this transition
- transition timetable and action plan summary

Guidance on how to complete the templates will be found alongside each template in Section 2 of this toolkit. Examples of how to use these templates are to be found in Section 3.

You may photocopy and/or adapt the blank templates in section 6 to meet your requirements but the remainder of the toolkit is subject to copyright restrictions. You can also find the templates on the CD-ROM at the back of the toolkit. The templates are available as PDF files, for you to print off and use, and as Word documents, for you to adapt as you wish.

Given everyone's busy workload, it is intended that the information gathered for inclusion in the plan is likely to be in existence, for example, from annual review reports, rather than something which always has to be created. The completed transition plan should also be used as a source of information for any staff who come into contact with the focus pupil.

Although there is a time/labour implication this needs to be balanced against the distress, confusion and anxiety which a young person with an ASC may suffer if planning is not in place. Given that a lack of planning often leads to challenging behaviours, it could be time well spent.

Transition plan

for

Name:

School:

Date of transition:

Pupil profile

{ *The aim of the pupil profile is to be a 'snapshot' view of the young person with an ASC that provides key information in an easy-to-read format.* }

Photograph of pupil

NAME:

DATE OF BIRTH:

NAME OF PARENTS/CARERS:

NAME OF SIGNIFICANT PEOPLE:

{ *This is useful for staff who are new to the young person, or who have infrequent contact, eg supply teacher, lunchtime supervisors.* }

ADDRESS:

TELEPHONE: EMERGENCY TELEPHONE:

E-MAIL:

SOCIAL WORKER: SUPPORT WORKER:

DIAGNOSIS/MEDICAL CONDITION:

MEDICATION:

MEDICAL PROTOCOL IN LINE WITH SCHOOL POLICY: { *Check the details required by the receiving school's medical policy and check information is consistent.* }

DIETARY NEEDS/LUNCHTIME ARRANGEMENTS:

{ *Include details of the pupil's dietary and support needs at lunchtime and snack times and guidance on how dietary needs are managed in food technology lessons.* }

SOCIAL SKILLS:

{ *Summarise the key social skills that the pupil finds difficult and any strategies that have been used successfully in the current school.* }

COMMUNICATION:

{ *Structure this into the pupil's level of understanding as well as their expressive language abilities. Try to give some examples to aid clarity.* }

BEHAVIOURAL NEEDS/LEVEL OF SUPERVISION:

{ *Summarise the behavioural management approach which is used and successful.* }

SENSORY ISSUES:

{ *Describe the sensory needs and the adaptations to the environment or situation that need to be made.* }

TOILET ARRANGEMENTS:

{ *Describe the levels of independence or support required.* }

PARENTAL PERMISSION GIVEN FOR ALL ACTIVITIES EXCEPT:

GENERAL:

{
This should include:

- *special interests or favoured activities which can be used as a calming/de-stressing activity, motivator or reward*
- *triggers to stress, anxiety and/or resultant challenging behaviour*
- *any 'obsessive' behaviours which indicate levels of stress/anxiety*
}

For information on curriculum strengths and difficulties and support needs see attached reports and pupil information relevant to this transition.

REPORT BY: **DATE:**

Summary of transition and key stakeholders

{ The aim of this template is to identify the type of transition and provide a contact list of the stakeholders involved in the planning process and completion of the transition. }

PUPIL: CURRENT SCHOOL:

TYPE OF TRANSITION OR CHANGE:

Home to early years placement	☐	Early years placement to school	☐
Class to class	☐	School to school	☐
Activity to activity	☐	Change of transport	☐
Other	☐		

DATE OF TRANSITION:

CHANGES LINKED TO THIS:

Key stakeholders involved in this transition

✓	Stakeholders	Name	Contact details
	Pupil		
	Parent/carer		
	SENCO		
	Current teacher		
	Current teaching assistant		
	New teacher		
	New teaching assistant		
	Key members of peer group		
	Lunchtime supervisor		
	LA support service		
	Health professionals		
	Social worker		
	Taxi driver and company		
	Taxi escort		
	Other		

{ Only include stakeholders relevant to this transition. This list is not exhaustive. Other stakeholders may need to be included. }

REPORT BY: DATE:

Identified training needs and support for staff

{ The aim of this template is to act as an assessment of training needs, the appropriate actions required to meet those needs and a record of who may deliver the training and what that may include. }

PUPIL: CURRENT SCHOOL:

Training for	Type of training/support	Training provider	Date of delivery and notes
Teachers All staff			
Teaching assistants			
Lunchtime supervisors			
Taxi drivers and escorts			
Peers			
Others *{ eg site manager, head of year, school librarian – personalise to receiving school }*			

Training and support can take many forms.

For example:

- *taught training sessions*
- *sharing of information – verbal and written*
- *shadowing previous members of staff*
- *observation of the pupil*
- *reading relevant books/articles*

There should be a minimum expectation that all staff who work with young people with an ASC should have received ASC awareness training. This training should include:

- *what an ASC is*
- *the implications for teaching and learning*
- *strategies to address the key areas of difficulty*

REPORT BY: DATE:

Pupil information relevant to this transition

{ This information should be collated in partnership with the young person with an ASC at the centre of the process. This information may already be available in alternative formats, for example in annual review or school reports. If so, it may not be necessary to rewrite it. Reports from outside support agencies should be incorporated into the grid or attached as supporting evidence. }

PUPIL:

In partnership with pupil, parents/carers, school and *{ This should identify any 'outside' professionals if involved }*

Area	Updated
Personal strengths:	
Personal difficulties:	
Communication (expressive and receptive):	
Social skills:	

Area	Updated
Curriculum strengths:	
Curriculum difficulties:	
Level of support required (curriculum and unstructured times):	
Extra curricular activities:	
Other:	
Reports available from outside agencies:	

For information on curriculum strengths and difficulties and support needs see attached reports and pupil information relevant to this transition.

REPORT BY: DATE:

Key strategies and resources for this transition

{ The aim of this template is to summarise the strategies and resources selected to support this particular transition. A list is provided as an aide-memoire. }

PUPIL:

Strategy/resource	Details	Person responsible	Notes
Additional visits to receiving placement			
Personal information booklet		*The lead person producing/ developing each resource should be identified.*	
Photographs			
Map			
Video/DVD			
Schedules/timetables			
Cue cards			
Social stories			
Comic strip conversations			
Symbols			
Pupil passport			
'Goodbye'/closure activity			
Other			

REPORT BY: DATE :

Transition timetable and action plan summary

The aim of this template is to summarise all planning information associated with the transition, placed in chronological order to aid implementation and to provide a checklist as the process progresses.

Refer to case study for example of how to use this section.

PUPIL:

Date	Action	Action by	Notes	Initial and date

REPORT BY: DATE :

Section 3

How to use the templates – case study examples

In this section you can find out:
- how to use the templates by referring to two case studies

Case study one

A case study for a young person with a diagnosis of an ASC and ADHD moving from Reception into Year 1 in a mainstream primary and nursery school.

This pupil is at the School Action Plus stage of the SEN Code of Practice.

While this case study is realistic, it is not based on actual people.

Not all the templates have been used in this case study. The ones selected match the individual's needs and the type of transition.

Transition plan

for

Name: Simon Billings

School: Holly Primary and Nursery

Date of transition: September 2007

SECTION 3   *How to use the templates – case study examples*

Pupil profile

NAME: Simon Billings

DATE OF BIRTH: 2.7.2001

NAME OF PARENTS/CARERS: Mr and Mrs Billings

NAME OF SIGNIFICANT PEOPLE: Ms Anderson – speech and language therapist, Mr Helligan – teaching assistant

ADDRESS: 12 Mead Close, Sunnydale, Bromsgrove B37 5ML

TELEPHONE: 0123 456789   **EMERGENCY TELEPHONE:** 07894 56123

E-MAIL: sjbillings@new.com

SOCIAL WORKER: Mrs Kendall   **SUPPORT WORKER:**

DIAGNOSIS/MEDICAL CONDITION: ASC and ADHD

MEDICATION: Ritalin

MEDICAL PROTOCOL IN LINE WITH SCHOOL POLICY: 1 tablet given at home at 8am by Mrs Billings.

DIETARY NEEDS/LUNCHTIME ARRANGEMENTS: Needs adult prompt to keep eating and a consistent seating arrangement in a quiet area of hall.

SOCIAL SKILLS: Simon is often on the periphery of school groups and finds it difficult to initiate approaches. He requires structured support to be successful. Simon finds large group work difficult and is best placed in a pair or group of three.

COMMUNICATION: Understanding: State Simon's name first to gain his attention. Speak clearly, using key words and short phrases. Use visual aids to support his understanding whenever possible. Be firm and consistent in your expectations. Implement cue cards to support Simon's understanding of daily routines ie morning, break time, lunchtime, home time, etc.

Expression: Simon can make most of his 'wants' known by short phrases.

BEHAVIOURAL NEEDS/LEVEL OF SUPERVISION: Simon has no sense of danger with regard to road safety. Hand must be held at all times when out of school.

Simon can demonstrate inappropriate and challenging behaviour if he becomes over-stimulated. This presents as a high-pitched squeal. Give clear instructions, avoid unnecessary language. Recognise trigger words, give Simon space.

SENSORY ISSUES: Sensitive to loud noises, especially in dining hall. Provide a set place on the edge of the room away from the general walkway. Sit with supportive peers if possible.

TOILET ARRANGEMENTS: Needs to be escorted to toilet first few times so that he knows where to go. Verbal reminders about going to toilet required occasionally.

PARENTAL PERMISSION GIVEN FOR ALL ACTIVITIES EXCEPT: Contact with animals. Simon has allergies to certain animals. He can be given antihistamine medication to alleviate symptoms, but parents must be consulted about all activities/outings where he may come into contact with animals.

GENERAL: Favoured activities: playing in water and trains. Both can be used as a reward, but use clear visual cue to show Simon when his turn has ended.

Uses visual timetable. The other children on Simon's table also use the timetable.

Reads all words seen but does not necessarily understand all meanings.

Fine motor skills – requires support in this area.

Simon has a special interest in his twizzler sticks. They are like brightly coloured pipe cleaners. He is allowed to bring one to school, but it stays in his bag, except for break and lunchtime. Make sure Mrs Billings knows if it is lost or damaged at school.

Simon responds to working at an independent worktable for some activities.

Simon uses a carpet square to sit on for group, carpet activities and assembly.

For information on curriculum strengths and difficulties and support needs see attached reports and pupil information relevant to this transition.

REPORT BY: Mrs Horton   DATE: 15 May 2007

Summary of transition and key stakeholders

PUPIL: Simon Billings   **CURRENT SCHOOL:** Holly Primary and Nursery

TYPE OF TRANSITION OR CHANGE:

Home to early years placement	☐	Early years placement to school	☐
Class to class	☑	School to school	☐
Activity to activity	☐	Change of transport	☐
Other	☐		

DATE OF TRANSITION: September 2007

CHANGES LINKED TO THIS: Simon will move from Reception to Year 1. He will also move onto the Year 1 and 2 playground, with new lunchtime supervisors.

Key stakeholders involved in this transition

✓	Stakeholders	Name	Contact details
✓	Pupil	Simon Billings	0123 456789
✓	Parent/carer	Mr and Mrs Billings (John and Judy)	0123 456789
✓	SENCO	Mrs Horton	0221 678 9123 mhorton@new.com
✓	Current teacher	Miss Trout	0221 467 8912 strout@new.com
	Current teaching assistant		
✓	New teacher	Mrs Jones	0121 567 8912 jjones@new.com
	New teaching assistant		
✓	Key members of peer group	Ann Smith, Katie Pitt, Jack Lewis, Dan Mule	School
✓	Lunchtime supervisor	Mrs Harris	School
✓	LA support service	Mrs Jenkins	0572 465342
✓	Health professionals	Ms Anderson (speech and language therapist)	0221 789 1234
✓	Social worker	Mrs Kendall	0572 56789
	Taxi driver and company		
	Taxi escort		
	Other		

REPORT BY: Mrs Horton   **DATE:** 15 May 2007

Identified training needs and support for staff

PUPIL: Simon Billings   CURRENT SCHOOL: Holly Primary and Nursery

Training for	Type of training/support	Training provider	Date of delivery and notes
Teachers All staff	ASC awareness, implications for teaching and learning and possible strategies	LA support service (Mrs Jenkins)	3 September 9.00 – 11.00 11.15 – 12.15 for teachers
Teaching assistants			
Lunchtime supervisors Mrs Harris	Current strategies used during Reception	SENCO	4 September
Taxi drivers and escorts			
Peers	ASC awareness and strategies that will assist Simon	Teacher and LA support services	Review at end of first half-term to assess need. Oct. 07
Others			

REPORT BY: Mrs Horton   DATE: 15 May 2007

Key strategies and resources for this transition

PUPIL: Simon Billings

Strategy/ resource	Details	Person responsible	Notes
Additional visits to receiving placement	Two visits to be made, in addition to school transition plan for all other pupils	Current teacher	
Personal information booklet	To include information about new rooms and staff to be encountered	Current teacher	
Photographs	Of new rooms, staff and routes. To be used in personal booklet	New teacher	
Map	Map not required but TA to walk Simon to new class and through new routes into class from playground	School TA	
Video/DVD	N/A		
Schedules/ timetables		New teacher	
Cue cards	'good listening' cards used		
Social stories	N/A		
Comic strip conversations	N/A		
Symbols	For schedule	New and current teacher	List possible symbols needed to be photocopied and laminated
Pupil passport	Not required for this transition		
'Goodbye'/closure activity	Miss Trout to say goodbye to Simon on last day and state his new teacher is Mrs Jones	Miss Trout	
Other	N/A		

REPORT BY: Mrs Horton   DATE: 15 May 2007

Transition timetable and action plan summary

PUPIL: Simon Billings

Date	Action	Action by	Notes	Initial and date
June 2007	Simon to spend some time in new class with school TA when class is empty	New class teacher	Take photos as you go to help him recall people and places later	
"	Begin to make up booklet of photographs to support understanding of changes	Current class teacher	Include schedule photographs ie morning routine, where to hang coat, put lunch box etc	
July 2007	Take Simon on short informal visits to new class to meet new teacher	Current class teacher	Take photos	
"	Simon to go with whole class to meet new teacher in new classroom	Current class teacher	Take photos	
"	Show Simon booklet of photographs and talk to him about changes	Current class teacher	Use a calendar to show when changes will happen	
"	On last day of term give Simon opportunity to say goodbye as his closure activity	Current class teacher	Take photos	
"	Booklet to go home to be read through the summer holiday	Parents	Ensure Simon understands that friends will be moving with him	

REPORT BY: Mrs Horton   DATE: 15 May 2007

Case study two

This case study is for a child with a diagnosis of an ASC moving from a mainstream primary school to a mainstream high school.

This pupil has a Statement of Educational Need and teaching assistant support for seven hours a week.

While this case study is realistic, it is not based on actual people.

Transition plan

for

Name: Edward Wilson

School: Beacon Primary and Nursery

Date of transition: September 2007

Pupil profile

NAME: Edward Wilson

DATE OF BIRTH: 24/6/95

NAME OF PARENTS/CARERS: Mr and Mrs Wilson

NAME OF SIGNIFICANT PEOPLE: Mrs Andrews (current TA)

ADDRESS: 27 Shortland Grove, Bromsgrove B35 8NW

TELEPHONE: 0221 457 1234   EMERGENCY TELEPHONE: 07899 12345

E-MAIL:

SOCIAL WORKER: N/A   SUPPORT WORKER: N/A

DIAGNOSIS/MEDICAL CONDITION: Autism Spectrum Condition

MEDICATION: Supplement programme (multi vitamins/minerals etc)

MEDICAL PROTOCOL IN LINE WITH SCHOOL POLICY: All medication administered at home

DIETARY NEEDS/LUNCHTIME ARRANGEMENTS: Gluten and casein free diet. Packed lunch from home provided. Needs adult support initially and the same seating place every day in a quiet area of canteen.

Liaise with home in advance of any lessons/activities involving food. Mrs Wilson will provide ingredients/adapted recipes if necessary. Contact her in advance (two weeks' notice if possible).

SOCIAL SKILLS: Edward finds social interaction with peers and unfamiliar adults a challenge. Once used to routine, he should be able to gain some independence moving around school, but in the larger environment this will be a slow process. Edward has responded to a buddy system.

COMMUNICATION: Expressive: Edward can make his needs known verbally. He will need prompts to remind him when and who to ask for help.

Receptive: He can respond to direct questions provided you have his attention: use his name first. Keep language simple and concrete. Give clear choices supported by visual prompts if possible.

BEHAVIOURAL NEEDS/LEVEL OF SUPERVISION: When Edward is stressed or anxious he can present with challenging behaviour. This may involve hitting himself or pushing others. Try to pre-empt by looking for the trigger of the stress/anxiety and modify the environment. Use positive language in a calming voice. Do not 'crowd' him. Direct Edward to a quiet area to calm. Wait 5 – 10 minutes before trying to engage with him.

SENSORY ISSUES: Needs to have clothes smooth (unruffled) against his skin, especially socks – the 'lines/ridges' need to be straight.

TOILET ARRANGEMENTS: Ensure Edward knows where toilets are situated in all areas of the school and which signs/symbols to look for. Edward will benefit from a social story to help explain appropriate times to go to the toilet, and to remind him about toilet etiquette ie, closing door behind you.

PARENTAL PERMISSION GIVEN FOR ALL ACTIVITIES EXCEPT: Activities involving food – see dietary needs. Discuss level of support to be provided for any out of school activities with parents in advance.

GENERAL: Calming activities and strategies:
Edward has a 'de-stress toolkit' which contains items that immediately make him calm. He knows it is kept in the Form Room.

Key triggers:
Noisy, echoing rooms ie, hall, dining room, gym.
Edward may require support before entry to these rooms.

Edward has a pupil passport for any member of staff to view to explain about himself.

For information on curriculum strengths and difficulties and support needs see attached reports and pupil information relevant to this transition.

REPORT BY: Miss Chilwell   **DATE:** June 2007

Summary of transition and key stakeholders

PUPIL: Edward Wilson **CURRENT SCHOOL:** Beacon Primary and Nursery

TYPE OF TRANSITION OR CHANGE:

Home to early years placement	☐	Early years placement to school	☐
Class to class	☐	School to school	☑
Activity to activity	☐	Change of transport	☑
Other	☐		

DATE OF TRANSITION: 5 September 07

CHANGES LINKED TO THIS: From Beacon Primary School to Wallace High School. Edward is able to access the Pupil Support Centre at Wallace High if necessary. A request is being made to the LA for transport arrangements to remain the same, as Edward is very familiar with his current driver and escort.

Key stakeholders involved in this transition

✓	Stakeholders	Name	Contact details
✓	Pupil	Edward Wilson	School
✓	Parent/carer	Mrs Wilson	0221 457 6666
✓	SENCO	Mrs Childs	0221 457 9876
✓	Current teacher	Miss Chilwell	0221 457 4567 across@worc.net
✓	Current teaching assistant	Mrs Andrews	0221 457 4567
✓	New teacher	Form tutor: Mr Hopwell Year head: Miss Sanders	0221 457 9876 bhopwell@worc.net
✓	New teaching assistant	Mrs Wells	0121 457 9876
✓	Key members of peer group	Circle of Friends – Kay Brown, David Kelly, Owen Foster, Jenny Evans	School
✓	Lunchtime supervisor	Mrs Murray	School
✓	LA support services	Mr Cox – EPS / Ms Richard – ASC support team	01905 36363
✓	Health professionals	Mr Patel – clinical psychologist Mrs Jacobs – speech and language therapist	01525 23456 01527 76543
	Social worker		
✓	Taxi driver and company	Mr George – Go Carefully Taxis	07899 767676
✓	Taxi escort	Mrs Grace	01527 91919
✓	Other	Mrs White	01905 45454

REPORT BY: Miss Chilwell **DATE:** June 2007

Identified training needs and support for staff

PUPIL: Edward Wilson   CURRENT SCHOOL: Beacon Primary and Nursery

Training for	Type of training/support	Training provider	Date of delivery and notes
Teachers All staff	All staff training – ASC awareness, implications for teaching and learning strategies	LA support service	1 morning – 3 hours
Teaching assistants	As above	LA support service	1 morning – 3 hours
Lunchtime supervisors	Include in whole staff training	As above	1 morning – 3 hours
Taxi drivers and escorts	It is hoped that Edward's current taxi and escort will continue, so no further training required	SENCO	Taxi driver/escort will need details of dropping off points and where to take Edward to before end of summer term
Peers	Continue with Circle of Friends	SENCO	It is vital that Edward continues to receive support from peers. Once he has settled it would be valuable to run a new Circle of Friends project to include some of his new peer group.
Others Subject teachers	Circulate transition plan information and current Individual Education Plan	SENCO to action	

REPORT BY: Miss Chilwell   DATE: June 2007

Pupil information relevant to this transition

PUPIL: Edward Wilson

In partnership with pupil, parents/carers, school and LA support service

Area	Updated
Personal strengths: Great sense of fun, delightful personality. Usually happy and co-operative if structure and warning of change is in place. Excellent rote memory, especially from tapes and videos. Good eye–hand co-ordination and balance. Will persevere with a task.	
Personal difficulties: Significant social and communication difficulties, especially in turn-taking situations. Finds rules of games difficult to learn and apply. Is nervous of sudden movements and unexpected noises.	
Communication (expressive and receptive): Is increasingly using questions appropriately. Ability to repair conversations and ask for clarification is also improving, although Edward continues to require answers to his questions in language that he can understand. When he becomes anxious his ability to process and retrieve words for use is compromised.	
Social skills: Edward likes to feel part of a group and his Circle of Friends have helped in this. He can often end up being too rough in his play or unintentionally rude to others. He often misinterprets others' intentions and perceives himself as being bullied.

Edward has recently joined an informal Saturday morning football club run by 'Dads' in Bromsgrove – he has limited understanding of the game. However, the members have been very supportive and it is rewarding to see Edward mix with some of the local children. | |

Area	Updated
Curriculum strengths: Edward demonstrates a great interest in history and is able to remember and recall many historical details. He is able to demonstrate his abilities when using a computer.	
Curriculum difficulties: Edward is making slow but steady progress with his functional literacy skills. His fine motor control and handwriting have improved, though he needs reminding to 'write neatly' when working independently. Edward finds the using and applying aspect of numeracy difficult.	
Level of support required (curriculum and unstructured times): When familiar with the setting, Edward is able to move around school independently. There are many sessions now where Edward does not require adult 1:1 support, eg PE, history, music, assembly and some literacy topics, etc.	
Extra curricular activities: Edward successfully participated in an after-school golf activity. Due to his prior understanding of golf, taught by Mr Wilson at home, and excellent peer support, Edward participated in and enjoyed the activities without any additional support from school staff.	
Other: Since the implementation of the Circle of Friends project Edward's awareness of others and his ability to engage and participate in activities has improved.	
Reports available from outside agencies: Pupil passport – Edward Wilson Speech and language therapy report – Ms Jacobs	

For information on curriculum strengths and difficulties and support needs see attached reports and pupil information relevant to this transition.

REPORT BY: Miss Chilwell				DATE: June 2007

Key strategies and resources for this transition

PUPIL: Edward Wilson

Strategy/ resource	Details	Person responsible	Notes
Additional visits to receiving placement	Three additional visits to be made, initially when other pupils are in lessons. Gain info to become familiar with key staff, rooms and routines	Current SENCO	
Personal information booklet	To be developed with Edward during his introductory visits	Current TA and new SENCO	Need digital camera
Photographs	Used to support the above	New SENCO	Summer term 2007
Map	Of key areas of new classroom and school Establish key routes	SENCO	To be used during introductory visits
Video/DVD	1. General video of school 2. Edward's personal video to be made during his introductory visits	Current teacher and TA	Summer term 2007
Schedules/ timetables	To be developed through current TA/teacher in liaison with new school, SENCO and base staff	Current teacher	Summer term 2007
Cue cards			
Social stories	Explain school move. Explain new school routines, eg start of day, lunchtime, end of day	Current teacher	Summer term 2007
Comic strip conversations			
Symbols			
Pupil passport	To use existing passport	Parent	
'Goodbye'/ closure activity	As part of the class leaving activity	Miss Chilwell	Photo of class given, goodbye written on it
Other Buddy support	Consider using Circle of Friends children to help Edward move around school	Current TA, new form tutor	

REPORT BY: Miss Chilwell   DATE: June 2007

Transition timetable and action plan summary

PUPIL: Edward Wilson

Date	Action	Action by	Notes	Initial and date
November 2006	Meeting at new school	Edward's parents, new school SENCO and head teacher		
January 2007	Current class teacher and TA visit to new school	New school SENCO and class teacher, current class teacher and TA		
March 2007 (at annual review)	Meeting to discuss transition arrangements, exchange of information, outside agency support required and to agree outline timetable for summer term 2007	Edward's parents, new school SENCO, current class teacher plus invited agencies		
Spring term	New school SENCO visits current school to meet Edward and discuss strategies, curriculum issues with current staff	New school SENCO, current class staff		
End spring term	Meeting to agree timetable for introductory visits during summer term	New school SENCO and form tutor, current class teacher and TA, parents		
Summer term	Series of supported, planned introductory visits	New form tutor, current TA, Edward		
Summer term	During visits photos, video and personal information booklet for Edward to be developed	New form tutor, current TA, Edward		
June/July 2007	ASC training for new school staff	LA support service		

SECTION 3   *How to use the templates – case study examples*   51

Date	Action	Action by	Notes	Initial and date
July 2007	Review meeting to: - Agree timetable for first few weeks, start and end of day, and those mainstream lessons which Edward may be able to access independently. - Special diet and implications for lunch time, food technology, etc. - Agree home school communication approach. - Discuss support arrangements throughout school day	New school SENCO and form tutor, current class teacher and TA, parents		
Summer holiday	Talk to Edward about transition using photographs, video and booklet	Parents and Edward		

REPORT BY: Miss Chilwell

DATE: June 2007

Section 4

Strategies and guidelines for successful transitions

In this section you can find out about:

- essential strategies:
  - additional visits to receiving placement
  - personal booklet of new information
  - pupil passports
  - visual aids
- other strategies:
  - social stories
  - comic strip conversations
  - buddy systems
  - Circle of Friends

Essential strategies

Additional visits to receiving placement

The following include a range of suggestions. It is important to select only the ones relevant for that young person. Where reference is made to a school, the same applies to other types of receiving placements (eg short-break, social care residential placements, etc).

- Additional visits to a receiving school should be timed to be when pupils are in lessons and the corridors are relatively empty. If support hours have been allocated and a teaching assistant (TA) has been identified at the receiving school, then the TA should be increasingly involved with the pupil on visits. These additional visits should begin *before* the formal, school-arranged induction visits.
- The focus pupil and one other can be the ones chosen to carry out 'the mission' to find information for the other pupils going to that school. They produce a book of information and then relay it back to a small group of pupils. This contains information about key staff, rooms and routines.
- Make/use a map of the school. Identify key places, ie form room, hall, office, playground, toilets, cloakroom/lockers, dining hall, library, subject rooms and transport collection point.
- Use the map in a game, ie take me to ... etc. Find a room number or block and link to the subject.
- Familiarise the young person with the school planner and link the above to the timetable. It is likely that the pupil will need to be taught how to use it.
- To help the pupil practise with the format of timetable used in the receiving school, use the same format in the existing school for the rest of the term. Some pupils may find it helpful to copy the existing timetable into the new school format so they understand how the new timetable format works.
- Teach the other purposes of the planner, ie for recording homework, writing notes, organisation and finding out which books and equipment are needed for a particular day. If possible use copies at the existing school to ensure familiarity.
- Using a camera – digital, if possible – make an information book of relevant rooms and key staff. Identify key places, ie form room, hall, office, playground, toilets, cloakroom/lockers, dining hall, library, subject rooms and transport collection point.
- Outline the first day, from arriving in the playground, and run through the routine (verbally and physically).
- Use role-play to develop 'what if?' scenarios.
- Establish named staff who can be approached if difficulties arise.
- Join in with routines that require particular skills or organisation, ie tuck time and lunch time (having to order, use money, etc).

- Through discussion (and Q & A) explore things the pupil is looking forward to and any queries they may have.
- Receiving school staff should visit and observe the pupil in the current setting.
- The current school should arrange a meeting with receiving school key staff in order to share information about the pupil, ie motivators, triggers, difficulties, etc.

Personal booklet of new information

- The pupil should be provided with a book of information about their new school or class. This book is intended as a visual aid to assist in their understanding of what is to happen and to familiarise them with the new people and places in their life.
- Identify key places ie new classroom, hall, office, playground, toilets, cloakroom/ peg, tray, hall, library and pick up/drop off point.
- Identify key staff – class teacher, teaching assistants, etc.
- Using a camera – digital if possible – present this information in the form of a book, ie of relevant rooms and key staff. Have a front and back cover and the pupil's name and picture on, eg 'Emma's new school and class'.
- Include one picture and one sentence on each page.
- This book should be read with the pupil, in school, up to the time of change.
- The completed book should also be sent home for it to be read regularly with the pupil. This is especially important when the change is from July to September.
- The book can be in the format most appropriate to the pupil – written, pictorial or perhaps a personal CD with pictures and text. (Hesmondhalgh & Breakey, 2001)

Pupil passports

A pupil passport is a way for parents or individuals to pass on important information about their child or themselves.

It is a collection of important and well-presented information about an individual with communication difficulties.

It was first used by Sally Miller at the CALL Centre, University of Edinburgh and developed by SENSE Scotland, through its project 'Use of Personal Passports with Deafblind People'.

The passport has been successfully used with people with an ASC.

Pupil passports should be devised between an adult (parent or member of staff) and young person.

Very young people with an ASC will vary in their level of input in providing information for the passport, depending on their ability to do so. Likewise their level of involvement in the production of the passport will vary.

The following two examples of passports are merely that. The passport on which example one was based was produced as an A5 booklet with colour clip art pictures throughout. We have illustrated the first two pages to show the effect of a passport with pictures. Some children find pictures distracting or confusing and so the remainder of the passport is text only, but uses a variety of fonts and type size, again as an illustration.

Example two is also text only, but produced in the format of small pieces of card that fit into a credit card type wallet, which could easily be carried in a pocket.

Suggested headings for writing a pupil passport

- A title for the front page
- Introduction:
  - My name is …
  - Important things about me are …
  - The most important things you need to know are …
- Important people
  - Family and friends
  - Important people and places
  - Contact details sheet
- Likes/dislikes:
  - How I express these
  - Things that may upset or frighten me
  - Things I like to do/am good at
  - Places I like to go
  - Things I like to eat and drink
- Communication:
  - I communicate through …
  - If I do this it means I …
  - To help me understand what you are saying …
- Achievements:
  - Things I can do for myself
  - Things I am learning to do
- Strategies:
  - Things I need someone else to do for me
  - How I work best and things you can do to help
  - If I am unhappy… (ways to comfort me)
  - Equipment I need and use
- Medical information
- Any other things you may want to include

Pupil passport example 1

At School, I love 6
- Science
- Mrs Perfect
- Running round with my friends
- History
- Soft snuggles
- ...and reading!

Hello, my name is...
Andrew
and I have...
lots of...
ENERGY!

Section 4   Strategies and guidelines for successful transitions

There are some things that I find very difficult.

- I don't always understand exactly what you mean when you tell me things.
- Unexpected changes worry me.
- I can't tell people apart by their faces, so sometimes I can't tell which of my friends is which.
- When I know a lot about something, all my thoughts turn into words and just come spilling out. I can't stop until I have said everything.
- Sometimes I answer rudely without realising it.
- Sometimes there are things I HAVE to do, even though I know I shouldn't. I can't stop, but it is often embarrassing and I hate it.

I hate

Writing

Waiting

Noise

Being told off and...

...when people don't believe me!

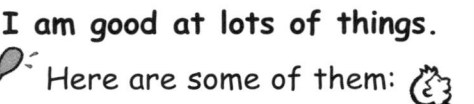

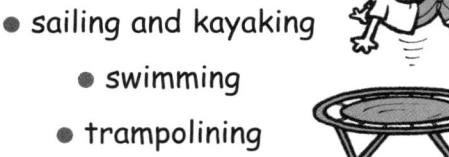

I am good at lots of things.

Here are some of them:

- sailing and kayaking
- swimming
- trampolining
- climbing trees
- making things with dad
- reading and maths

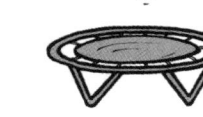

60 Transition toolkit

If I twitch or make little squeaky coughing noises, these are my tics.

I call them my Tourettes. They happen most when I am **excited** or **worried**. I can't help them and I can't stop them, so please don't ask me to.

If I am ticcing a lot, I may need to use my **'time-out' card**, or I may be soothed by a cloth **'Snuggle'** from my special bag or box.

Occasionally I have horrid tics that make me spit, kick, swear or choke.

I am trying hard to get even better at lots of things.

Here are some of them:

- **waiting** for my turn to speak
- **singing**
- putting up my **hand**
- **writing**
- **typing** at the computer
- showing I'm **sorry**

My ADHD makes it very easy for other people to distract me, wind me up and get me into trouble.

If this is happening,

PLEASE HELP ME TO CALM DOWN!

Time-out, **snuggles**, a quiet time with a **book** or a **drink** of water may help.

When I have to suck my shirt, it gets wet and uncomfy.

I have **spare shirts** in my bag.

Mum had to buy a new washing machine to get my shirts clean!

Contact details

Home: 01905 18345

Mum's mobile: 07855 236567

Mum's work: 01905 34563

Dad's mobile: 07767 47671

Granny: 01905 56722

Doctor: 01905 67023

My friend's mum: 01299 712355

I need to take tablets every day, which make it easier for me to concentrate and think. I take a Dexedrine 5mg tablet three times a day. If I need a tablet while I am with you, mummy or Mrs Perfect will have arranged it. I usually take my tablets at breakfast-time, lunch-time and tea-time. I also take melatonin capsules at night.

I know that everyone is different and that everyone is special.

I know that my disabilities make it hard for people to understand me.

Thank you for reading this, and for helping me.

Further information is available from the following organisations:

ADHD
National Attention Deficit Disorder Information and Support Service
www.addiss.co.uk

Asperger Syndrome
The National Autistic Society www.nas.org.uk

Tourette Syndrome
Tourette Syndrome Support www.tsa.org.uk

Comments

This is a working, ongoing document. We can add to it, remove bits and generally update it as necessary.

If you have any suggestions or comments to make about the contents or format of this file, we would be pleased if you'd write them below, so that we can change things if we need to.

date	comment	name

Thank you

Cynthia and Andrew Child

Pupil passport example 2

This is Pravina's passport.

The information in here is very important to Pravina.

Please follow the suggestions made.

The information may not seem important to you. However, if you do not follow it, it can have devastating effects on Pravina.

My name is Pravina Shah
Call me Pravina
Things you should know

Signed: Pupil

Signed: Parent

Signed: Teacher

Dinner time

I am allowed to go in on first dinner sitting with a friend because I can't eat very quickly and I worry about it.

Signed:

Lunch supervisor

Things you should know

- I like milk and water but not fizzy drinks
- I like bread, chips, fish fingers and ketchup

Lesson time

- Copying from the board is difficult for me
  Please let me copy something on the table
- I find it difficult to do things fast or under pressure
- Please help me copy down my homework details

Lesson time

- I find other people's systems confusing
- I am sometimes confused by instructions
- I find cutting, colouring and some art skills difficult
- I find handwriting difficult
  Please give me extra time to work things out

Lesson time

- I find noises, movements and computers distracting.
  Please sit me away from these
- If I lose concentration in my work
  Please touch me on the shoulder, look at me and point down, rather than saying my name

---

PE

- I have a problem with co-ordination
- It takes me longer to get changed and I have trouble with my buttons, socks and laces
  Please give me extra time and some help with my buttons
- I am worried about the shower

Playtime

Please don't keep me in over playtime, as I need to move, run and talk to be able to concentrate in the next lesson

- I often think I'm going to get knocked over
  Please help me if I feel I am being picked on

SECTION 4   Strategies and guidelines for successful transitions

Important things • I don't like shouting, crowds, noise, fires, sad or frightening things on the television – sometimes I panic *I will calm down if I'm not forced to do something* • When you shout at other pupils I can think that you are shouting at me *Please let me know you are not*	**Important things** • I find it difficult to look people in the eye. I can't concentrate on what they are saying if I am made to *Please accept me not making eye contact* *or* *If on a 1:1 basis, you could remind me by tapping me on the shoulder and pointing at your eyes*
Important things • I don't like being in front of a big audience or showing things to people I don't know *I am happy to demonstrate what I have worked out myself, to a known audience* • I get confused by some instructions or lots of instructions together *Please give me extra time to work things through*	**Around school** • I find rushing about school worrying • Sometimes I can't get past people in the corridors or worry that I will be late for lessons *Please don't tell me to 'hurry up' too often because it makes me make more mistakes and then be late*
What I like and can do well • I am a very good reader • I like to read about machines • I like to draw detailed diagrams (but not colour them in) • I can do tick box tests quickly	**What I like and can do well** • I may need extra time if I need to write a long answer • I like calm things to look at and to listen to eg water movement, the colour blue, natural things and anything that gently and continually moves – *These help me to be calm*
Important people • Mum, Mrs Jones and my friend Mary *I am allowed to talk to Mrs Jones in school, please let me go to find her when I need to.* *If Mrs Jones is not available I can go to Mr Davies*	**Contacts** Mum: 0123 891234 Dad: 0987 654321 Ellen Clements: childminder 0325 554221

Visual aids

Individuals with an ASC learn in a variety of ways, as do most people of typical development. However experience has shown that many people with an ASC learn best using visually presented information and cues. It is this increased understanding of the unique patterns of learning associated with ASCs that has shown us one of the most successful strategies for use with young people with an ASC – that of presenting information in a visually structured way.

Visual aids help young people with an ASC to understand their world better. However the medium used must match the young person's ability/developmental level. It is important to keep visual support clear and concise, including only the precise information necessary to complete a task.

Visual cues can be used to achieve success in a variety of circumstances, eg to complete tasks, to understand rules and routines, to understand what is expected or to give information.

The visual cues selected can take a variety of styles from real objects and photographs through to line drawings, symbols and words – representing a continuum of levels of abstraction that are clearly linked to the individual's level of understanding.

Figure 2: Examples of visual supports for a schedule

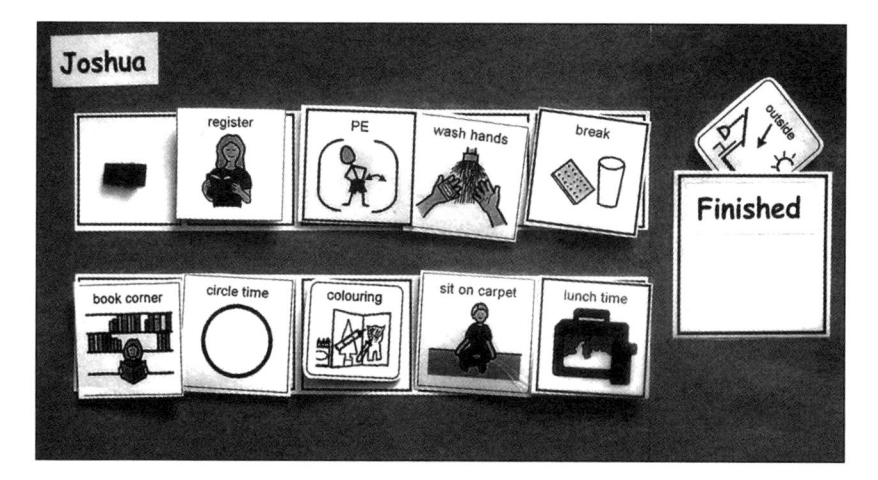

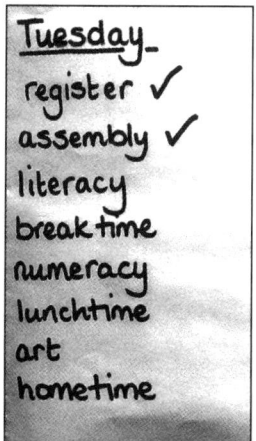

These three examples of one use of visual supports – that of a schedule – highlight the simplicity of the design and the variety of styles available.

Photographs

Any type of camera can be used, although digital cameras offer editing opportunities that conventional cameras do not have. Ensure that the photograph you take encapsulates the message you wish to impart, with the focus being in the centre of the picture.

Symbols

Several companies make icons (line drawings that are either black/white or coloured) that can be photocopied. Boardmaker (Mayer-Johnson, 1981) and Writing with Symbols 2000 (Mayer-Johnson, 2000) are examples of commercially made icons.

Other strategies

Social stories

Individuals with an ASC experience a range of social skills and social understanding difficulties at home, school and in the wider community.

There are a wide range of strategies and published social skills programmes to aid the teaching of the necessary social skills and strategies. One such approach, developed by Carol Gray (1994a), is the use of social stories.

Social stories were devised to provide individuals with an ASC with accurate information regarding situations they encounter and appropriate responses to social situations. They are presented in a format which takes into account an individual's attention span and the need for information to be presented in a clear, concise manner.

Each story provides information about a specific social situation – about why it is happening and what a typical response might be. This is done in an explicit overt way. Research has shown that individuals with an ASC are not able to pick up on the incidental information embedded in social situations with the same ease as individuals of typical development.

Guidelines for writing social stories

The following are brief guidelines for writing social stories. For more information refer to Gray (1994a).

Many people are deterred from using social stories because at first sight they don't seem easy to write. However, they are a powerful tool and it is worth 'having a go' as soon as possible to address an issue, rather than worrying about writing a perfect social story.

Bear these rules in mind, remembering that rules can be broken.

A social story is divided into three sections:

- descriptive sentences – these are facts and set the scene
- perspective sentences – describe the perspective of other people
- directive sentences – to change the behaviour

Remember, a social story is:

- personal
- visual
- permanent
- written in simple language
- based on careful assessments
- explicit
- focused on an area of core need
- factual
- focused on what people are thinking and feeling
- one that holds meaning
- accurate
- not insulting
- written using a formula

Keep the child central to the story and have a specific goal in mind. A series of stories may be required.

Gather the information with the child as this will create a tangible story.

Do not write the story with the child present. Write a draft story and review it with another adult who also knows the child.

Use the formula of six sentences to one directive sentence. (However it is possible to have a fabulous social story with no directive sentences in it.)

Type or write the story in as clear a way as possible leaving as much white space on the page as possible.

Read the story daily at a particular time of day. Stories should also be read immediately prior to the situation to which an amendment in behaviour is required.

Spend up to fifteen minutes of 'special one-to-one time' devoted to the child during which the story is read. Read the story, talk and enjoy the time together.

Read the story several times (until you and/or the child are bored).

Only move on to the next story once an improvement in the current targeted behaviour has been observed.

Revisit previous social stories if required.

Stories may be stored in a book or ring binder. If this is done, write a list of 'contents'. Write the child's name and the first title. Add the stories one by one. Update the contents list every time a new story is added.

Use a calendar (perhaps with the social story book) to record events which can be discussed in 'special time' with the child.

Explain the aim of the stories to the child and that the stories may be read to them daily if possible. Explain that the book is special and private.

The following examples explain the social story as a model and cannot be considered 'true social stories'. They do, however, show the flexibility of the approach to match the situation.

Social story example 1

A social story to explain a change of class to a young girl with an ASC

At school, children work in different classes.

This year I am in Mr Jones's class.

Sometimes we have had a story in Mrs Hart's classroom.
After the summer holiday, I will change classes and be in Mrs Hart's class.
All the other children will move classes too. The children in my class will be the same children.

The new classroom looks different. Mrs Hart may do things differently and the timetable will not be the same. We will have a different cloakroom too.

I may be nervous when I start my new class in September. Other children will be nervous too. They will be uncertain where to go and what to do. They may ask an adult for help.

I will try to remember what to do by looking at the photographs of my new class and checking on my timetable.

If I am not sure what to do I will try to ask Mrs Hart. Mrs Hart is there to help me.

Social story example 2

A social story to explain a change to the morning routine at school

Different classes do things at different times and in different ways.

In my new class I will have a new routine to go into school. Other children may feel confused by this at first. I may find it confusing too.

If I get confused I can watch the other children or ask someone to help me.

When I come to school in the morning, I carry my own bag.

Mum will say 'Goodbye' and leave me at the school gate. I will say 'Goodbye' to mum and go to the top playground.

When I get to the top playground, I will put my bag on the floor like the other children.

Continued

I will look for my friends and other children in my class. They may be looking for me. I will try to say 'Hello' to them and play with them.

There will be a teacher on the playground. They are there to help me if I need it.

When the teacher says 'Go in now' I will pick up my bag and go into school.

- Say 'Hello' to my teacher and my friends.
- Hang up my coat and take my lunch box and water bottle out of my bag.
- Put my lunch box on the shelf and my water bottle on my table.
- Put my reading folder in my drawer.
- Sit down on my chair and listen to the teacher.

Social story example 3

A social story to explain a change to the home time routine at school

When we change classes we need to do some things differently.

I am used to a certain routine at the end of school. When I am in my new class this will be different.

The teacher will tell us what to do. I may find it confusing. Other children may find it confusing too. We can watch and help each other.

When the teacher says it is time to go home, I will put my things away in my drawer and tidy my table.

I will put my lunch box, water bottle and reading folder in my school bag and listen to my teacher.

When my teacher tells me to get my coat, I will fetch my bag and my coat from the cloakroom and line up with the other children.

My teacher will lead us to the playground.

I will say 'Bye' to my friends and look for my mum.

When I see her I will tell my teacher and go straight to my mum to go home.

Comic strip conversations

'A comic strip conversation is a conversation between two or more people which incorporates the use of simple drawings. These drawings serve to illustrate an ongoing communication, providing additional support to individuals who struggle to comprehend the quick exchange of information which occurs in a conversation.' (p1)

'Comic strip conversations may be used in conjunction with social stories or independently to solve the problems a student encounters.' (p14) (Gray, 1994b)

The following are brief guidelines for composing comic strip conversations. For more information refer to Gray (1994b).

The choice of materials

- White boards have the advantage that changes can easily be made and erased, but no record can be kept.
- Interactive white boards with a printing facility are ideal: they have the advantages of white boards and the option to keep a hard copy of the conversation.
- Paper is very versatile and offers permanence, but it is difficult to erase drawings made in colour.

Introducing a comic strip conversation

- Before introducing comic strip conversations to a young person, practise to ensure you can draw easily while talking.
- Introduce the session by saying something like 'let's draw as we talk today'.
- Divide large boards/pieces of paper into frames and encourage the young person to draw from left to right in sequence.
- Let the young person take the lead and encourage them to write/draw/talk the majority of the time. At first you may ask questions as in an interview, but gradually the format should become more like a conversation.
- Sit side by side with joint attention on the conversation work area.
- Start with small talk to indicate its importance in social conversation, eg the weather or the weekend. The weather in particular is easy to draw and so can build confidence.

- Guide the young person's drawings with questions, eg 'Where were you?', 'Who was with you?', 'What happened?', 'What did you say?', 'What did others think when they said/did that?'. The adult's goal is to achieve a balance between gathering insights into the young person's perspective, while sharing accurate social information.

- Encourage a sequence in the conversation by using boxes and suggesting the young person numbers them. If using paper, these boxes can be cut apart and rearranged.

- Use colour in conversations for emotional content. Gray (1994b) has developed a colour chart listing suggested colours and associated motivations and feelings, eg green: good ideas, happy, friendly; red: bad ideas, teasing, anger, unfriendly. Introduce the colours one at a time over several conversations. Gradually a combination of colours can be used to represent conflicting emotions.

- Review key points in the conversation and encourage the young person to summarise it.

- To conclude the conversation, identify new solutions. If the young person cannot generate them, suggest possible solutions. Encourage the young person to create a numbered plan from the suggested solutions.

Using a dictionary

Gray (1994b) has developed a Comic Strip Conversation Dictionary, which contains eight symbols for basic concepts including: listening, interrupting, loud, quiet, talk and thoughts. These can be used to aid consistency between conversations and the symbols can be gradually introduced as the student gains in confidence. She also recommends that the young person develops their own personal symbols dictionary with symbols for specific people, places and concepts which are part of the student's personal experience. It is important that the symbols are simple and quick to draw to keep conversations flowing. Building up a set of consistent symbols personalises the approach and gives the young person control over their communication system.

Buddy systems

'Having a "buddy system" for playtimes and breaks can help as both protection and for teaching the pupil with an ASD ways of interacting more successfully with others.'
(Jordan & Jones, 1999)

Buddy systems can take many forms. The essence is for one or more of the peers of the pupil with an ASC to provide buddy support to the pupil through all or part of the school day. The buddies may:

- accompany the pupil between lessons to ensure they know where to go and what they need
- assist during lessons
- act as a friend at playtime or a lunchtime companion

A very effective example of buddy support was developed by a specialist teaching assistant in one mainstream school with an autism base for pupils with ASCs. In PE lessons two buddies provided a 'sandwich' for one of the base pupils. One of the buddies went in front of the pupil with an ASC to model what the pupil should be doing next, for example on the apparatus. The other buddy stayed behind the pupil, talking quietly to encourage the pupil to stay on task, watch the activity being modelled and to prompt the pupil to take his turn at the right time.

The same 'sandwich' technique was also used in assemblies, on sports day and during a three-day residential school trip attended by the pupil. Observation of the pupil on sports day showed him actively looking for his buddies, so that he could position himself in the 'sandwich', which provided security and support without the need for adult intervention.

The buddies should be given some basic training in the difficulties faced by children with an ASC and guidance in how best to help the particular pupil, for example 'make sure you say his name first'; 'use simple language'; 'don't worry if he doesn't respond at first'; 'do not touch him without warning' and an understanding of any particular triggers to be avoided. They should also be encouraged to model appropriate forms of behaviour for the pupil. The buddies must also know who they can go to if they need help. It is important to avoid giving too much responsibility to just one or two buddies. The ideal scenario is to start with a few supportive peers and gradually build up the number of peers who can provide effective and unobtrusive buddy support.

With older pupils, providing buddy support may enable adult support to be reduced and so may increase the pupil's feelings of independence. A buddy scheme also provides valuable experience to the buddies, by raising their awareness of disability and promoting an understanding of how they can help and support others.

Circle of Friends

Circles of Friends have been described as a way of providing:

> 'practical support for the children with autism, while gaining benefits for peers, all with minimal costs, and minimal drawbacks for any participants' (Jordan & Jones, 1999)

> 'practical and emotional support for the pupil during work and leisure activities within and outside school' (Jordan & Jones, 1999)

The 'Circle of Friends' approach is now often used in the UK to assist able pupils with an ASC to develop their social and communication skills (Newton et al, 1996; Letheren Jones, 1999).

The approach seeks to help the peer group to develop an understanding of the focus child's difficulties and encourages the peers to reflect on how they might feel if they faced the same problems. It encourages peers to identify and implement their own helping strategies. The focus child is given the chance to become part of a group in the structured settings of the Circle meetings and also outside Circle meetings, but still with support from the supervising staff.

The followings steps are recommended when setting up and running circles (Newton et al 1996; Taylor, 1997; Whitaker et al, 1998):

- The process starts with a whole class meeting to discuss the focus child's difficulties and strengths and to think of ways that they can be helped by their peers. The parents' and focus child's consent to this meeting is sought, but the focus child does not attend.
- The first session ends by the group leader asking for volunteers to join a smaller circle of six to eight friends for the focus child.
- There follow six to eight weekly half hour meetings between the Circle children and the focus child, with a key member of staff acting as the facilitator. The main purpose of the meetings is to generate supportive ideas and practical tactics to assist the focus child. The focus child can also express their concerns in this supportive environment and develop links with other children. Building the self-esteem of the group is a vital element of these meetings and the facilitator should seek to encourage mutual support, trust, openness and honesty among group members (Newton et al, 1996).
- During the project the Circle children report back to the rest of the class about the Circle meetings and any strategies identified.
- At the end of the agreed period, the formal Circle sessions stop and the children are left to continue supporting the focus child using the strategies they have developed for themselves during the project (Bozic et al, 2002).

Section 5

Further reading and references

In this section you will find:

- a review of current literature on managing change and transitions for children with an ASC up to the age of twelve
- strategies for managing change and transition for children with an ASC
- types of transition
- references

Review of current literature

This review draws together the advice and strategies contained in the research and current literature relating to managing change and transitions for children with an ASC up to the age of twelve years. The review:

- highlights the main issues and recommendations
- gives an overview of the strategies for managing change and transitions for children with an ASC

The review concentrates on work published since 2000 and also some important previous texts. It encompasses articles from professional journals and advice from local education authorities and voluntary organisations. While no single work on this subject has been identified, all the referenced texts include some useful advice.

Literature to improve understanding of autism

One of the essential components for enabling smoother transitions and understanding why change is so difficult for people with an ASC is to grasp the fundamental differences in perceiving and making sense of the world around them for people who have autism and those who do not. Having an awareness of yourself, of what makes you similar to others and what makes you different and feeling valued for who you are, rather than what you are not, is the bedrock of self esteem and self worth. Some key texts that explore themes around developing self-awareness and managing personal emotions are included in the reference section.

Personal accounts, including those by Sainsbury (2000) and Jackson (2002) offer the reader vital insights into what it means to have an ASC and to feel different and excluded as a result. Other authors, for example, Welton (2004), Doherty, McNally and Sherrard (2005), attempt to give siblings, peers and/or the young person with the diagnosis of ASC a better understanding of the differences between the world of autism and the neurotypical world, so that they can co-exist more harmoniously and the difficulties of transition and change for someone with an ASC can be more easily recognised and managed by those on both sides of the spectrum.

Faherty (2000), Vermeulen (2000), Plummer (2001) and Korin (2006) all take a workbook approach to enabling young people with ASC to work through activities that will help them, stage by stage, to come to an understanding of themselves and to feel proud of who they are rather than becoming anxious and stressed because they cannot cope with change and transitions like everybody else can. Attwood (2004) uses the same kind of individual, activity based, workbook approach to help young people with ASC to manage their anger and anxiety, while the work of Dunn Buron (2003, 2007) makes use of the idea of a five point scale as a visual way of understanding and managing emotions.

Recent literature illustrating tried and tested strategies

Larkey (2005) provides practical strategies and worksheets for improvement of play and social skills, general behaviour and subject difficulties such as reading, writing and maths. She also makes suggestions for dealing with the constant questioning that may arise from anxiety and uncertainty and for managing obsessions and special interests.

Beaney and Kershaw (2003 and 2006) also provide photocopiable support materials for use in primary and secondary classrooms respectively, addressing issues around adapting the curriculum and the learning environment, using visual support and promoting positive behaviour through the use of strategies such as social stories. Examples are given of appropriate IEP targets, behaviour support plans, pupil profiles and reward systems to improve motivation.

Hewitt (2006) provides a practical guide to the concept of life story books, a development of the idea of the 'communication passport', which helps staff understand the background and diverse strengths and challenges of each individual, as well as helping the individual in question to understand their own progress.

The whole series of books in the Autistic Spectrum Disorders Support Kit by Attfield, Bowen, Morgan and Plimley (2006–07) address issues around transition in every age and ability group from early years to secondary school. They offer some very practical suggestions, backed up by current research, to teachers, classroom assistants and families supporting children and young people with ASC across a variety of settings.

The books by Brown and Miller (2003) and Baker (2005) set out clear examples of how to use schedules, planners and flowcharts to manage daily changes and transitions and to become more organised and less anxious. Brown and Miller (2003) address themes, including managing social relationships, the concept of time, work experience and independent travel, through logical questioning (e.g. what do I need to know? how can I find out?) and visual planning. Baker (2005) uses a direct conversational style to give essential information to the young person with ASC about topics such as non-verbal communication, seeing somebody else's point of view, conversational skills and stress management, alongside role play activities to practise these skills, so that anxiety can be reduced and transitions into unfamiliar situations managed more effectively.

No discrete guidelines on the subject of managing change and transitions have been found in the literature reviewed. However, the Department for Education and Skills and the Department of Health publication, *Autistic Spectrum Disorders: Good Practice Guidance* (2002), gives useful advice to schools on this subject. Philip Whitaker gives general guidelines on planning for change in his book *Challenging Behaviour and Autism: Making Sense – Making Progress* (2001) and Rita Jordan and Glenys Jones in their book *Meeting the Needs of Children with Autism* (1999) offer authoritative advice and valuable strategies for use in schools.

Main issues and recommendations

The main issues on managing change and transitions from the literature are:

- the importance of training for all staff who come into contact with pupils with an ASC
- liaison between teachers from school year to school year and between schools at phase transfers
- the need for a structured environment, both in terms of some level of physical structure and in structuring the school day and activities
- access to visual supports
- the need for schools to be flexible in their responses to individual pupil needs regarding changes and transitions, using a range of strategies, including social stories, to support pupils

Strategies for managing change and transitions for children with an ASC

Whole school strategies

When planning to welcome a pupil with an autism spectrum condition (ASC) (NIASA, 2003) a whole school understanding and awareness of the implications of ASC is of vital importance (Hodgson, 1997). A minimum requirement for all staff is a basic knowledge of the triad of impairments and their educational implications (West Midland SEN Regional Partnership, 2001). This understanding is a first step in selecting accommodations, interventions and environmental supports that can ensure educational and social progress (Smith-Myles & Simpson, 2002). All staff will need basic information on the particular needs of the pupil with an ASC (Jordan & Jones, 1999). This training should also be a requirement for lunchtime supervisors, bus escorts and students on work placements as these people often have the opportunity to contribute to the education of the pupil (Jones, 2000).

Setting up a safe haven/quiet room that is available at any time of the school day provides a retreat where pupils can go if they feel anxious, insecure or distressed (DfES & DoH, 2002). Pupils can be given a card to carry in all lessons and, if the card is shown to staff, the pupil is immediately allowed to leave the lesson and go to the safe haven (Whitaker, 2001). Lunch time clubs are particularly valuable (Harrison, 1998), as they offer pupils with an ASC the chance to play games and interact with other children under structured and safe conditions. Other appropriate break-time activities can also be offered and taught in these clubs (DfES & DoH, 2002), or pupils can prepare for future lessons or read their own social stories.

Rules are useful in supporting pupils through transitions (eg 'in the high school it is the rule that ...', etc). Because rules are neutral they allow for an appeal to an objective standard and so reduce the need for confrontation (Cumine et al, 1998). However, the rules will need to be applied more flexibly than for the rest of the pupils, as the needs and abilities to conform will be different for pupils with an ASC. A series of social stories to explain why people sometimes bend or break rules (Leicester City Council & Leicestershire County Council, 1998) can be written to help pupils understand other people's behaviours in this area.

Classroom strategies

An organised environment with a clear structure and a predictable daily routine (Connor 1999; Cumine et al, 1998; Wing, 1996) will enable pupils with an ASC to feel confident and safe in the classroom. Teachers need to try to maintain a sense of continuity and particularly to show consistency in their personal behaviour towards children (Smith, 1998; Jordan & Powell, 1995). The SPELL approach from the National Autistic Society gives an holistic framework for supporting pupils with an ASC that builds confidence and security, making pupils better able to deal with changes.

SPELL stands for:

Structure: structure makes the world a more predictable, accessible and safer place

Positive: positive approaches and expectations

Empathy: it is essential to see the world from the standpoint of the child with an autistic spectrum condition

Low arousal: the approaches and environment need to be calm and ordered in such a way as to reduce anxiety and aid concentration; and

Links: strong links between the various components of the person's life or therapeutic programme will promote and sustain essential consistency

(National Autistic Society, 2001)

Allocate specific activities to specific environments or areas of the room and direct the pupil to where the activity is to take place (Clements & Zarkowska, 2000). It is helpful to children with an ASC for the different areas of the classroom to be clearly labelled according to their uses, and for these designations then to be adhered to as often as is practical (Archer, 2004). Organising the learning environment into defined, clearly labelled areas will encourage children to learn the appropriate expected behaviours (Beaney & Kershaw, 2003). Where and how the furniture is placed can affect each pupil's ability to deal with the environment, understand its expectations and function independently. Designate seating positions within the classroom and allow the pupil to keep the same tray or drawer throughout the year (Cumine et al, 1998). It will be beneficial if the child's need for personal space is respected and individual working space allowed (Archer, 2004). Areas in the classroom where there is not as much activity are good to locate and establish as places for pupils with an ASC to work (Mesibov & Howley, 2003).

Some pupils with an ASC have abnormal responses to sensory stimuli; triggers for these responses include physical space (including personal space), levels of noise, lighting and lack of structure. When considering the environment for including pupils with an ASC, these factors need to be taken into account and possible remedies sought. It may not be possible to eliminate the environmental trigger, for example, the echoing of a school gymnasium, and so a planned programme of graded exposure to the trigger may need to be introduced (Maclean-Wood, 2003).

Where pupils find it difficult to make the transition from one activity to another, plan for the pupil to have short periods of involvement, with required activities interspersed with activities they particularly enjoy (Seach et al, 2002). Give a time limit for requests and instructions, eg 'Hang your coat up by the time I count to ten' or use a sand timer for timing clearing away at the end of a lesson (Cumine et al, 2000). Build up positive associations before exposing the pupil to change. Involve the pupil in an activity they find pleasurable or relaxing. It may be possible to continue this activity while the pupil copes with the situation (Whitaker, 2001). Prepare pupils for any changes well in advance and have a contingency plan for emergencies – a special activity or a favourite object (Evans, 2000).

Explain in detail how the pupil still can make contact with their teacher or teaching assistant whenever there is a need (a signal or special, 'secret' word), during changes in routine. Provide warning of impending changes or switch of activity (Connor, 1999) and tell the pupil what they should do within the changed routine (Jones, 2002). Tell the pupil what will happen and what they should do after the unexpected event (Herefordshire Educational Psychology Service, 2000). Have a special toy, place or activity for when unexpected change occurs (Lawson, 2001). When creating individual, written timetables for more able pupils, write in pencil so that regular changes can be easily introduced. In order to avoid a framework becoming a cage, it is important to introduce regular, planned changes to routines (Whitaker, 2001).

The TEACCH approach (Treatment and Education of Autistic and Related Communication Handicapped Children) gives the high degree of predictability to the pupil's day which some pupils need, with the use of physical structure, visual supports and schedules. The system also allows for the visible alteration of a sequence of events so that the pupil is not suddenly exposed to sudden change. The TEACCH schedules tell the pupil the sequence of the day's events, how to change from one activity to the next, what activity has been done, what activity remains to be done and when preferred activities will take place (Mesibov, 1997).

Give clear, consistent and concise instructions (Lawson, 2001) preferably with an additional visual support. Introducing lessons with a visual emphasis removes the need for the children to be reliant solely on an auditory input and leads to greater clarification of the concept being taught (Beaney & Kershaw, 2003). Use graded change techniques by gradually changing minor aspects of a situation, event, or activity, one step at a time. The changes should be made predictable for the pupil using visual cues (Howlin & Rutter, 1987). The changes can then be increased flexibly (Whitaker, 2001) and the pupils will build up a tolerance of uncertainty. Be alert to new obsessions and rituals, and build up gradual, small changes within the routines before they become too fixed (Whitaker, 2001). When statements are made which cannot be guaranteed, this should be made clear by adding 'probably' or 'maybe', and by teaching pupils what these words mean (Sainsbury, 2000).

Teach the concept of time using clocks, schedules or a diary. Pupils can then determine when specific events will occur and the sequence of activities throughout the day (Attwood, 1998). Teach the child the meaning of 'finished' and reinforce with an object of reference, sign or symbol (Connor, 1999). Visual or other sensory cues will help the pupil understand start and end points of activities (Clements & Zarkowska, 2000). There should be clearly marked areas to place finished work, even for the most able pupils (Mesibov & Howley, 2003).

Social stories (Gray, 1994a) will enhance the child's understanding of a situation or event (Rowe, 1999) and allow the teacher to focus on the relevant and immediate social difficulties being experienced by the pupil (Smith, 2001). Social stories can include photographs and drawings for younger children. The stories can be put onto tape to give independent access to non-readers (Autism Working Group, 2002).

Role-play or comic strip conversations (Gray, 1994b) provide children with 'scripts' to enable them to cope with anticipated new or changed situations they are likely to find difficult (Aarons & Gittens, 1998). Giving a pupil a set of rules 'for one day only' can support them through a short period of change (Powell, 2002). For older pupils a one-off behaviour contract could be useful. The contract should indicate the anticipated change, how the pupil should behave, who will monitor the pupil and the reinforcement/reward. The pupil and teacher then review the document and both sign it when the teacher is certain the pupil understands. The pupil can take the contract to the new situation and refer to it as necessary (Smith-Myles & Simpson, 1998).

A 'work buddy' or Circle of Friends (Newton & Wilson, 1999) can support a pupil with an ASC through changes in classroom routines, both by staying with the pupil and by giving appropriate models of behaviour. A mat or carpet square can be helpful to show the pupil where to sit or stand in new situations (Jordan & Jones, 1999).

Regular physical exercise during the day can help children manage their anxiety (Clements & Zarkoska, 2000, and Lawson, 2001), increase stamina and help the child to understand rhythm and routine (Roberts, 1999) and break lessons up into more manageable periods of time.

Visual supports

Children with an ASC have stronger visual than auditory skills and, even when children can understand verbal instructions, these need to be supplemented by visual information (Wall, 1998). The use of objects, photographs, pictures and symbols will help children 'see' processes and sequences of events (Lawson, 2001). For pupils who require more concrete visual cues to understand forthcoming events, a schedule can be devised that uses actual materials from the scheduled activities (Smith-Myles & Simpson, 1998). Pupils can learn their daily schedules by feeling objects for a few minutes before the relevant activity, eg fifteen minutes before lunch, give the pupil a fork to hold; let them hold a toy vehicle for a few minutes before going out in the car (Grandin, 1995), or give the child a toilet roll prior to going to the toilet.

Include the pupil's rituals/obsessions in their individual timetable (Whitaker, 2001). Variations in routine can be effected by providing external representations of stages, eg a set of written steps, pictures or objects which can be manipulated by changing one of the steps and so allowing the pupil to prepare for the change (Jordan & Powell, 1995). Colour coding, numbering, naming or sorting according to types, products placement, belongings, time of day, etc (Lawson, 2001) will help children know where something fits and where to put displaced items. This knowledge will make them feel more secure within the class and more able to tolerate changes in routine.

Pictograms can illustrate activities such as reading, numbers etc and introduce children to the concept of 'what comes next' (Aarons & Gittens, 1998). Use a separate card for each activity attached to a board using blu-tack or velcro. Should there be an unexpected change, the cards can then be rearranged (Attwood, 1998). It is important to share control and involve pupils in planning their own schedules (Sainsbury, 2000). Pupils may enjoy and sometimes feel more comfortable when they participate in the preparation of their schedule. Ideally, this participation should occur first thing in the morning. Pupils can assist in assembling their schedule, copying it or adding their own personal touch. This interactive time can also be used to review the daily routine, discuss changes and reinforce rules (Smith-Myles & Preston, 1998). Allowing the pupil to make shifts in the order of the cards on his own timetable will help him to become accustomed to the prospect of changes (Connor, 1998).

In addition to a class timetable explained in photographs or symbols, pupils can have individual timetables using a mixture of photos, symbols, words and/or objects, depending on their level of understanding. These can be displayed in the pupil's workstation to give instant reference about what is to happen next (Tutt & Cook, 2000). Individual visual timetables should cover a time span appropriate for the pupil's abilities: activity, lesson, part-day, day, etc. The timetable can be colour coded to highlight specific events (Clements & Zarkowska, 2000); for example, literacy could be green and maths could be blue. Red could signify time to go the toilet and yellow for play. The pupil needs to understand the connection between the particular card and the activity it stands for (Herefordshire Educational Psychological Service, 2000). It is important to check that the pupil actually understands their timetable through careful assessment of their reactions to individual symbols or pictures (Potter & Whittaker, 2001).

Pupils should interact with their individual timetables, crossing off completed activities or removing cards and putting them into a 'finished' box (Clements & Zarkowska, 2000). A 'surprise', 'mystery', blank or question mark card can be used to accustom pupils to unexpected events (Clements & Zarkowska, 2000). The visual timetable can include favourite objects, free time or preferred activities. These will encourage pupils to complete the required tasks (Jordan & Powell, 1995) by building in rewards. Teach a 'disappointment routine' – what to do when things do not go as expected (Clements & Zarkowska, 2000). Checking schedules regularly can also facilitate transitions as the schedules provide a comfortable, predictable and consistent routine for pupils. They help to make the process of changing from one activity to another easier and less likely to provoke anxiety (Mesibov & Howley, 2003).

A time line can be used to show children how long a session will last or on how many occasions a particular activity will be repeated. The time line can be in the form of a long strip of card, marked out in the days of the week, with the relevant days highlighted in a different colour. An appropriate picture – a van, a frog, a train, etc – is then moved from one highlighted day to the next at the end of every session. This gives the child a visual representation of time passing and helps them to anticipate the future (Aarons & Gittens, 1998).

For older, more able pupils who can cope with information a long way ahead, calendars and diaries can be used to 'count down' towards important events. The pupil is then prompted to cross off or tear out a page each day (Clements & Zarkowska, 2000). However, for some pupils, a prolonged period of anticipation could make them even more anxious (Jordan & Jones, 1999). Clock faces can be adapted to make them easier to read. The minute and second hands can be removed and pictures and symbols fixed around the clock. Hour glasses or kitchen timers help the pupil see time passing (Clements & Zarkowska, 2000). Using two clocks, one with the 'now' time and the hands on the other put 'then' – the time of the end of the session or activity – is useful to mark the end of a session (Parker, 2000).

The visual timetable and individual workstations can be transferred to other classrooms, providing continuity and security to pupils until they no longer need them (Tutt & Cook, 2000).

Types of transition

Transitions between classes and schools

The Year 5 annual review is a crucial time to plan the transition to secondary school and allocate responsibilities for managing the process. It is important that the Year 7 co-ordinator and the SENCO from the high school attend this meeting. The transition plan to the next class should include observations by the new teacher of the pupil and discussions with the current teacher of strategies and approaches that have been successful. The transition plan can include a social story with photographs and visits to the new setting (Hannah, 2001). Teachers and support staff from both schools meet to discuss how to facilitate the transition (Attwood, 1998).

An induction pack could be prepared for the new teacher/school which would include a general fact file about ASCs. This would help to create a consistent approach which meets the needs of the pupil and where staff can feel confident and supported to meet the demands presented (Jones, 2000). The school leadership team needs to be aware of likely difficulties arising from rotation of staff, placement of student teachers and maternity leave disrupting the pupil's routine (Attwood, 1998).

Some secondary schools organise their Year 7 and Year 8 separately from the upper school thus making for a more sheltered start which would better support the transition of pupils with an ASC. The Year 6 class of the primary school could follow a programme of work in the summer term that would be continued in Year 7, eg Herefordshire pupils work on a science passport in Year 6 that is taken with them and continued in their high school.

An early exchange of accurate and up-to-date records, profiles and ways of working with the child between the primary and secondary school (DfES & DoH, 2002) will support planning and ease the transition. Make the pupil aware of the impending transfer well in advance and prepare a book of photographs about the children to be in their new class, with their names and what they like doing (Seach et al, 2002). Arrange additional visits for pupil and parents at different times of the school day, including when no other children are there (DfES & DoH, 2002). The pupil could also spend one afternoon each week in the new class/school for the previous term before transfer, accompanied by a teaching assistant and/or a small group of friends. Moving through a school and into new phases with a group of chronological peers that the pupil knows creates a constant situation that will support the pupil through changes and transitions (Pleven & Jones, 2000). Allow the pupil to wear the uniform of the new school on the induction visits and during the school holiday.

A 'passport' or pupil profile could be created with the pupil and their parents. The passport could give a pen portrait of the pupil with the more specific individual information that adults new to the classroom might need, including information about how to help the pupil learn. This would be a way of imparting this relevant information to colleagues quickly and the pupil could be involved in preparing the passport (Jones, 2000).

A teaching assistant could transfer with the pupil to the new class or school for the first term (Pleven & Jones, 2000). A teaching assistant from the secondary school could also visit the pupil in the primary school once a week for the previous half term (Seach et al, 2002). A link member of staff or key worker in the new school should have responsibility for managing the transfer and would be available for the pupil to discuss any concerns.

Secondary schools need to develop methods of disseminating information to all staff who will come into contact with the pupil (DfES & DoH, 2002, and Attwood, 1998). Visual information about the new class or school can be given to the pupil and their family in the form of photographs, a video, and/or a timetable. The video could show the different areas of the school at different times of the day and be shown to the child at home over the summer holiday before transfer. The pupil could be involved in collecting information about the new school into a 'new school file' during the final term of Year 6. A plan or map of the school, to carry around in a pocket or bag (Harrison, 1998) will give added security for some pupils. A personal handbook could be prepared which sets out solutions to everyday problems, such as who to ask for help with work, what to do if you get lost in school, and what to do at the end of the school day. As well as this practical information, the handbook could give strategies on what the child could do if feeling anxious or sad at school (Christie & Fiddler, 2001). Older pupils would benefit from having the following term/year's timetable before the end of the term.

The study of another language, such as French or German, in the new secondary school could throw up certain challenges for pupils with an ASC. They may have difficulties understanding that the same object could have another name in another language and in understanding that other people can communicate in different languages (Llacer & Jordan, 2003).

Transitions within a school and between activities

Have a transition ritual that is gone through after one activity is completed and before the next one begins, eg breathing exercise, physical exercise (a Brain Gym activity is ideal), a particular piece of music or song or a special object (Clements & Zarkowska, 2000). Brain Gym movements can be used as 'brain break' activities to focus children first thing in the morning, after lunch and during lessons (Heath, 2003). Pupils could be allowed to take a favourite object or a bag of 'twiddlers' with them between lessons (Whitaker, 2001) as a support through transitions, and where possible, reward all successful transitions (Rigg, 2002). New staff will need to be prepared and informed of the particular needs of the child (DfES & DoH, 2002).

A buddy scheme or Circle of Friends will support a pupil in class and break/lunch times (DfES & DoH, 2002). A Circle of Friends approach is a means of mobilising practical support for pupils while gaining benefits for peers, all with minimum costs and minimal drawbacks for any participants (Eddis, 2002; Whitaker, 1998).

Literally 'walking through' the timetable will help pupils to learn the routes around the school (Rigg, 2002). Clear signs, symbols or photographs in communal areas and subject bases (DfES & DoH, 2002) will enable pupils to be more independent when moving around the school. Give pupils checklists of equipment needed for different subjects/lessons (Harrison, 1998) rather than expecting them to remember. Allowing the pupil with an ASC to leave classes five minutes earlier or later with another pupil or pupils means they can avoid busy transition times (DfES & DoH, 2002; Jordan & Jones, 1999). A 'proximal control device', such as a personal stereo to use during transitions, gives pupils control over auditory stimulation and could help them cope in busy and noisy corridors (Jordan, 2002).

Opportunities for quality pastoral time at the end of the school day are valuable to check homework and discuss any issues that may have arisen which are causing concern (Rigg, 2002).

References

Publications that give a good introduction to ASC are highlighted by an asterisk.

Aarons, M and Gittens, T (1998)
Autism: A Social Skills Approach for Children and Adolescents
London: Wilmslow

Archer, M (ed) (2004)
'SEN: A Classroom Guide' *Special Children*
January/February 2004 Insert to journal

Attfield, E and Morgan, H (2006)
Living with Autistic Spectrum Disorders
London: Paul Chapman Publishing

* Attwood, T (1998)
Asperger's Syndrome: A Guide for Parents and Professionals
London: Jessica Kingsley

Attwood, T (2004)
Exploring Feelings: Cognitive Behaviour Therapy to Manage Anger
Arlington, Texas: Future Horizons

Attwood, T and Gillberg, C (2004)
'Developments in autistic spectrum disorders – influences for strategy and practice'
Wales First International Autism Conference, Cardiff, May 2004

Autism Working Group (2002)
Autistic Spectrum Disorders: A Guide to Classroom Practice
Belfast: Northern Ireland Department of Education

Baker, J (2005)
Preparing For Life: The Complete Guide For Transitioning To Adulthood For Those With Autism and Asperger's Syndrome
Arlington, Texas: Future Horizons

Beaney, J and Kershaw, P (2003)
Inclusion in the Primary Classroom: Support Materials For Children With Autistic Spectrum Disorders
London: NAS Publications

Beaney, J and Kershaw, P (2003)
'Positive Thinking Skills'
Special Summer 2003 12–15

Beaney, J and Kershaw, P (2006)
Inclusion in the Secondary School: Support Materials For Children With Autistic Spectrum Disorders (ASD)
London: NAS Publications

Bowen, M and Plimley, L (2006)
Autistic Spectrum Disorders in the Secondary School
London: Paul Chapman Publishing

Bowen, M and Plimley, L (2006)
Supporting Pupils with Autistic Spectrum Disorders
London: Paul Chapman Publishing

Bowen, M and Plimley, L (2007)
Social Skills and Autistic Spectrum Disorders
London: Paul Chapman Publishing

Bowen, M, Morgan, H and Plimley, L (2007)
Autistic Spectrum Disorders in the Early Years
London: Paul Chapman Publishing

Bozic, N, Croft, A and Mason-Williams, T (2002)
'A peer support project for an eight-year-old boy with an autistic spectrum disorder: an adaptation and extension of the Circle of Friends approach'
Good Autism Practice 3 (1) 22–30

Brown, M and Miller, A (2003)
Aspects of Aspergers: Success in the Teens and Twenties
London: Paul Chapman Publishing

Christie, P and Fiddler, R (2001)
'A continuum of provision for a continuum of need: opportunities for mainstream integration and inclusion provided by a specialist school for children with autism' *Good Autism Practice* 2 (1) 35–44

Clements, J and Zarkowska, E (2000)
Behavioural Concerns and Autistic Spectrum Disorders
London: Jessica Kingsley

Connor, M (1998)
Autism: Current Issues
www.mugsy.org

Connor, M (1999)
'Children on the Autistic Spectrum:
Guidelines into Practice'
Support for Learning 14 (2) 80–86

* Cumine, V, Leach, J and Stevenson, G (1998)
Asperger Syndrome: A Practical Guide for Teachers
London: David Fulton

* Cumine, V, Leach, J and Stevenson, G (2000)
Autism in the Early Years
London: David Fulton

Department for Education and Skills (2001)
Special Educational Needs Code of Practice
Nottingham: DfES Publications

Department for Education and Skills and
Department of Health (2002)
Autistic Spectrum Disorders: Good Practice Guidance
Nottingham: DfES Publications

Doherty, K, McNally, P and Sherrard, E (2005)
I Have Autism ... What's That?
Northern Ireland: South Eastern Education
and Library Board

Dunn, W, Myles, BS and Orr, S (2002)
'Sensory processing issues associated with
Asperger syndrome: a preliminary
investigation'
American Journal of Occupational Therapy,
56, 97–102

Dunn Buron, K (2003)
When My Autism Gets Too Big
Shawnee Mission, Kansas:
Autism Asperger Publishing Company

Dunn Buron, K (2007)
A 5 Is Against The Law
Shawnee Mission, Kansas:
Autism Asperger Publishing Company

Dunn Buron, K (2007)
A 5 Could Make Me Lose Control
Shawnee Mission, Kansas:
Autism Asperger Publishing Company

Dunn Buron, K and Curtis, M (2003)
The Incredible 5 Point Scale
Shawnee Mission, Kansas:
Autism Asperger Publishing Company

Eddis, M (2002)
'Circles of Friends: a qualitative study of this
technique with a ten-year-old child with an
autistic spectrum disorder'
Good Autism Practice 3 (1) 31–36

Evans, L (2000)
'Asperger Syndrome'
Special September 2000 21

Faherty, C (2000)
Asperger's ... What Does It Mean To Me?
Arlington, Texas: Future Horizons

Grandin, T (1995)
'How people with autism think', in Schopler, E and
Mesibov, GB (eds) *Learning and Cognition in Autism*
New York: Plenum Press

Gray, C (1994a)
The Social Story Book
Arlington, Texas: Future Horizons

Gray, C (1994b)
Comic Strip Conversations
Arlington, Texas: Future Horizons

Hannah, L (2001)
*Teaching Young Children with Autistic Spectrum
Disorder to Learn: a Practical Guide for Parents and
Staff in Mainstream Schools and Nurseries*
London: National Autistic Society

Harrison, J (1998)
'Improving learning opportunities in
mainstream secondary schools and colleges
for students on the autistic spectrum'
British Journal of Special Education 25 (4) 179–181

Heath, A (2003)
'Gym Lesson'
Special Autumn 2003 8–11

Herefordshire Educational
Psychology Service (2000)
*The Child with Asperger Syndrome in the
Ordinary School – a Guide for Teachers*
Herefordshire Education Directorate

Hesmondhalgh, M and Breakey, C (2001)
*Access and Inclusion for Children with
Autistic Spectrum Disorders 'Let Me In'*
London: Jessica Kingsley

Hewitt, H (2006)
Life Story Books For People With Learning Disabilities: A Practical Guide
Kidderminster: BILD Publications

Hodgson, A (1997)
'A Year with David'
Special Summer 1997 8-9

Howlin, P and Rutter, M (1987)
Treatment of Autistic Children
London: Wiley

Jackson, L (2002)
Freaks, Geeks and Asperger Syndrome: A User Guide To Adolescence
London: Jessica Kingsley

Jones, G (2000)
'Passports to children with autism'
Good Autism Practice 1 (1) 56–65

Jones, G (2002)
Educational Provision for Children with Autism and Asperger Syndrome
London: David Fulton

Jordan, R (2002)
Lecture notes from ASD for Mainstream Teachers course at Birmingham University

* Jordan, R and Jones, G (1999)
Meeting the Needs of Children with Autism
London: David Fulton

Jordan, R and Powell, S (1995)
Understanding and Teaching Children with Autism
London: Wiley

Korin, E (2006)
Asperger Syndrome An Owner's Manual: What You, Your Parents and Your Teachers Need to Know
Shawnee Mission, Kansas: Autism Asperger Publishing Company

Larkey, S (2005)
Making It A Success: Practical Strategies and Worksheets For Teaching Students With Autism Spectrum Disorder
London: Jessica Kingsley

Lawson, W (2001)
Understanding and Working with the Spectrum of Autism
London: Jessica Kingsley

Leicester City Council and Leicestershire County Council (1998)
Asperger Syndrome – Practical Strategies for the Classroom
London: National Autistic Society

Letheren Jones, M (1999)
Circle of Friends (video training pack)
Essex County Council Learning Services

Llacer, V and Jordan, R (2003)
Changing countries and languages: preparation for transition
Good Autism Practice, 4 (2) 27–35

Maclean-Wood, A (2003)
'Challenging behaviour: understanding and prevention'
Good Autism Practice 4 (2) 21–26

Mayer-Johnson, Inc (1981–2003)
Boardmaker CA, Solana Beach, USA: Mayer-Johnson, Inc

Mesibov, GB (1997)
'Formal and informal measures of the effectiveness of the TEACCH program'
Autism: the International Journal of Research and Practice 1 (1) 25–35

Mesibov, GB and Howley, M (2003)
Accessing the Curriculum for Pupils with Autistic Spectrum Disorders
London: David Fulton Publishers

National Autistic Society (2001)
Approaches to Autism: an easy guide to many and varied approaches to autism
London: The National Autistic Society

National Initiative for Autism: Screening and Assessment (NIASA) (2003)
National Autism Plan for Children
London: The National Autistic Society

Newton, C, Taylor, G and Wilson, D (1996)
Circles of Friends: an inclusive approach to meeting emotional and behavioural needs
Educational Psychology in Practice 11 (4) 41–48

Newton, C and Wilson, D (1999)
Circles of Friends
Dunstable: Folens

Outreach Support Service for Mainstream Education (2004)
Autism Initiatives: Greater Merseyside Pupil Transition Workbook www.autismtoolkit.com

Parker, M (2000)
'Setting up a base for secondary age pupils with an autistic spectrum disorder within a mainstream school'
Good Autism Practice 1 (2) 62-70

Pleven, S and Jones, G (2000)
'Inclusion: a positive experience for all'
Good Autism Practice 1 (2) 8-16

Plummer, D (2001)
Helping Children to Build Self-Esteem
London: Jessica Kingsley

Potter, C and Whittaker, C (2001)
Enabling Communication in Children with Autism
London: Jessica Kingsley

Powell, S (2002)
Supporting a Child with Autism
Kidderminster: British Institute of Learning Disabilities

Rigg, M (2002)
'Educational Issues for the Child with Asperger Syndrome'
Good Autism Practice 3 (2) 29-34

Roberts, G (1999)
'Supportive Frameworks'
Special Autumn 1999 22-25

Rowe, C (1999)
'Do Social Stories benefit children with autism in mainstream primary schools?'
British Journal of Special Education 26 (1) 12-14

Sainsbury, C (2000)
Martian in the Playground
Bristol: Lucky Duck Publishing

Seach, D, Lloyd, M and Preston M (2002)
Supporting Children with Autism in Mainstream Schools
Birmingham: Questions Publishing

Smith, C (2001)
'Using social stories with children with autistic spectrum disorders; an evaluation'
Good Autism Practice 2 (1) 16-25

Smith, P (1998)
'Stretched to the Limit'
Special Children June/July 1998 10-12

Smith-Myles, B and Simpson, RL (1998)
Asperger Syndrome: A Guide for Educators and Parents
Austin, Texas: Pro-Ed Publishing

Smith-Myles, B and Simpson, RL (2002)
'Asperger Syndrome: An Overview of Characteristics'
Focus on Autism and other Developmental Disabilities 17 (3) 132-137

Taylor, G (1997)
'Community building in schools: developing a circle of friends'
Educational and Child Psychology 14 (3) 45-50

Tutt, R and Cook, J (2000)
'Welcome to My World'
Special Children Issue 126 24-27

Vermeulen, P (2000)
I Am Special: Introducing Children and Young People to Their Autistic Spectrum Disorder
London: Jessica Kingsley

Wall, J (1998)
TEACCH training course notes
Sunfield School, Clent

Welton, J (2004)
Can I Tell You About Asperger Syndrome? A Guide For Friends And Family
London: Jessica Kingsley

West Midland SEN Regional Partnership (2001)
Report on Autistic Spectrum Disorders – Executive Summary
Birmingham: West Midlands SEN Regional Partnership

Whitaker, P (1998)
'Children with autism and peer group support'
British Journal of Special Education 25 (2) 60-64

Whitaker, P (2001)
Challenging Behaviours and Autism: Making Sense, Making Progress
London: National Autistic Society

Whitaker, P, Barratt, P, Joy, H, Potter, M and Thomas, G (1998)
'Children with autism and peer group support'
British Journal of Special Education 25 (2) 60–64

* Wing, L (1996)
The Autistic Spectrum: A Guide for Parents and Professionals
London: Constable

Section 6

Templates

In this section you will find the following templates:

- Transition plan cover page
- Pupil profile
- Summary of transition and key stakeholders
- Identified training needs and support for staff
- Pupil information relevant to this transition
- Key strategies and resources for this transition
- Transition timetable and action plan summary

The templates in this section may be photocopied or adapted to meet your requirements. You will also find the templates on the CD-ROM that accompanies this book. They are available as PDF files for you to print off and use and as Word documents for you to adapt as necessary.

Transition plan

for

Name:

School:

Date of transition:

Pupil profile

```
Photograph
of pupil
```

NAME:

DATE OF BIRTH:

NAME OF PARENTS/CARERS:

NAME OF SIGNIFICANT PEOPLE:

ADDRESS:

TELEPHONE: EMERGENCY TELEPHONE:

E-MAIL:

SOCIAL WORKER: SUPPORT WORKER:

DIAGNOSIS/MEDICAL CONDITION:

MEDICATION:

MEDICAL PROTOCOL IN LINE WITH SCHOOL POLICY:

DIETARY NEEDS/LUNCHTIME ARRANGEMENTS:

SOCIAL SKILLS:

COMMUNICATION:

BEHAVIOURAL NEEDS/LEVEL OF SUPERVISION:

SENSORY ISSUES:

TOILET ARRANGEMENTS:

PARENTAL PERMISSION GIVEN FOR ALL ACTIVITIES EXCEPT:

GENERAL:

For information on curriculum strengths and difficulties and support needs see attached reports and pupil information relevant to this transition.

REPORT BY: DATE:

Summary of transition and key stakeholders

PUPIL: CURRENT SCHOOL:

TYPE OF TRANSITION OR CHANGE:
Home to early years placement	☐	Early years placement to school	☐
Class to class	☐	School to school	☐
Activity to activity	☐	Change of transport	☐
Other	☐		

DATE OF TRANSITION:

CHANGES LINKED TO THIS:

Key stakeholders involved in this transition

✓	Stakeholders	Name	Contact details
	Pupil		
	Parent/carer		
	SENCO		
	Current teacher		
	Current teaching assistant		
	New teacher		
	New teaching assistant		
	Key members of peer group		
	Lunchtime supervisor		
	LA support service		
	Health professionals		
	Social worker		
	Taxi driver and company		
	Taxi escort		
	Other		

REPORT BY: DATE:

Identified training needs and support for staff

PUPIL: CURRENT SCHOOL:

Training for	Type of training/support	Training provider	Date of delivery and notes
Teachers All staff			
Teaching assistants			
Lunchtime supervisors			
Taxi drivers and escorts			
Peers			
Others			

REPORT BY: DATE:

Pupil information relevant to this transition

PUPIL:

In partnership with pupil, parents/carers, school and

Area	Updated
Personal strengths:	
Personal difficulties:	
Communication (expressive and receptive):	
Social skills:	

Area	Updated
Curriculum strengths:	
Curriculum difficulties:	
Level of support required (curriculum and unstructured times):	
Extra curricular activities:	
Other:	
Reports available from outside agencies:	

For information on curriculum strengths and difficulties and support needs see attached reports and pupil information relevant to this transition.

REPORT BY: **DATE:**

Key strategies and resources for this transition

PUPIL:

Strategy/resource	Details	Person responsible	Notes
Additional visits to receiving placement			
Personal information booklet			
Photographs			
Map			
Video/DVD			
Schedules/timetables			
Cue cards			
Social stories			
Comic strip conversations			
Symbols			
Pupil passport			
'Goodbye'/closure activity			
Other			

REPORT BY: DATE:

Transition timetable and action plan summary

PUPIL:

Date	Action	Action by	Notes	Initial and date

REPORT BY: DATE: